Don't You Dare Give Up

Don't You Dare Give Up

Renon Klossner Hulet

Deseret Book Company
Salt Lake City, Utah

Library of Congress Cataloging-in-Publication Data

Hulet, Renon Klossner, 1949–
    Don't you dare give up : the courageous comeback of Diane
Ellingson, All-American gymnast / Renon Klossner Hulet.
        p.   cm.
    ISBN 0-87579-531-5
    1. Ellingson, Diane.   2. Gymnasts—United States—Biography.
3. Paralytics—United States—Biography.   I. Title.
GV460.2.E45H85   1991
796.44'092—dc20
[B]   91-27607
                                                                           CIP

Printed in the United States of America
10   9   8   7   6   5   4   3   2

To our parents, Diane's and mine,
who are always there

Chapter 1

Diane Ellingson unpacked her bags, methodically setting out the things she would need for tomorrow, a habit she had developed long ago when she first started gymnastics.

She made her bed and flopped back against the petrified-foam pillow. The bed, too, was flat and leaden. Shower pipes groaned, and the sound traveled through the walls as if being conducted through water. She had been in dozens of dormitory rooms just like this throughout her career, and they all had the same smell: pink liquid makeup, Fritos, and copy machine ink. What made this dorm room feel different, though, was its loneliness.

Being alone on tour was a major change from the pattern of Diane's life. She was on her own for the first time in twenty-two years. Growing up securely sandwiched into the middle of a family of seven children, Diane had for most of her life been one of many on a gymnastics team. But today, just two weeks before Christmas 1981, she had boarded the airplane to Florida without family or coach or team. For the first time in her life she was a gymnast without cheerleaders.

She reached into her purse and pulled out a letter. The return address read: "The United States Professional Gymnastics Classic." Diane smiled. Some of the best gymnasts in the country were on this tour, and she felt honored to be one of them. The tour was the brainchild of Kurt Thomas, a world champion gymnast and a member of the 1972 Olympic team. The show, co-sponsored by Madison Square Garden, was to be an extravaganza, a "Holiday on Ice" featuring gymnastics. It was to run thirteen weeks with forty-nine performances across the country. With salary, per diem, expenses, and prize money, Diane stood to make at least fourteen thousand dollars, money she needed to finish college now that her gymnastics scholarship had been used up. She planned to have her teaching degree in a year.

Diane had announced her retirement from gymnastics at the end of the season with the University of Utah the previous spring, but when Kurt called her six months later to join the show, she decided that would be an even more fantastic way to finish up a career. But trying to get back into gymnastics so quickly, without having worked out all summer, was not the smartest idea. The first thing she did was pull a groin muscle while trying to learn a handspring front on the vaulting horse, the only event she was not confident in. Diane wanted Kurt's faith in her to be justified—there were dozens of other gymnasts he could have invited on the tour, and she didn't want to be the weak link. She was determined to learn that move—and now she almost had it. She just couldn't quite make the full somersault to land on her feet without a spotter.

"I'll have it by tomorrow afternoon, though," she thought,

giving the pillow a plumping. She was comfortable now. Fatigue took hold and lulled her slowly to sleep. She was running, jumping on the spring board, pushing through position in a handstand on the vaulting horse, and from there, pushing off into the highest, most beautiful one-and-a-half somersault anyone ever saw, landing on her feet, performing the move perfectly.

The next morning she met the others at the gym for orientation. She already knew some of the people; others she knew by reputation. The air was electric with talent. Some minutes into the meeting, every head turned toward the door when Marcia Frederick, the hottest gymnast in the country, sauntered in.

Diane's eyes narrowed thoughtfully. Marcia Frederick was good. Some said unbeatable. But no one is really unbeatable, Diane thought. Surely somebody could beat Marcia Frederick, and she might as well be the one.

Diane was enthralled by the atmosphere of rehearsal. She smiled, laughed, joked, and teased, and the others caught the heat of her enthusiasm. She picked up the moves and rhythms rapidly. Two hours flew by in a clamor of music, the choreographers yelling, and dozens of workers pounding scenery together. Finally, the rehearsal broke up. Diane and the others lay flat on their backs on the floor, panting.

"What a ball," said Diane to no one in particular. "I love this."

When Kurt Thomas called the women together for a meeting in the locker room, Diane was excluded. Wondering why, she went through the dance routines in her head. Had she done something wrong? Finally, the others came back into the gym, none of them looking any too happy.

"What was that all about?" she asked.

"He told us we're fat, and we have to lose weight."

Diane fought back a grin. Gymnasts are notoriously critical of each other's weight, and Diane had dieted all summer.

In the late afternoon, she worked on bars and beam first, and then begged Kurt Thomas's coach to help her with the vaulting horse. She was still determined to learn the hand-spring front before the day was out.

"You have to get plenty of air taking off to execute the one-and-a-half," the coach said. "Why don't you try a few timers first? Push off the horse in the vault, think about the somersault, but don't do it."

"Right," said Diane.

"Good," he said when Diane, completing her first timer, rolled forward on the mat as if she were a parachutist breaking the force of landing. "You went really high. You'll have plenty of time to rotate and land on your feet. Now, try it with the somersault."

Diane ran, jumped, and pushed off hard, but instead of waiting for her body to reach the apex, she immediately tucked her head under for the somersault.

The coach dived in on his knees, grabbed Diane under the shoulders, and flipped her so that she landed on the floor on her back. "Wow! You undercut your front. You're going to hurt yourself that way," he said.

"Okay. I'll do another timer."

It was perfect.

"Okay," said the coach. "Now, do the somersault. Push harder off your hands and wait on it."

Diane ran, pushed off, but once again ducked her head too soon. The coach reached in and broke her fall.

"Hey," someone called from the other side of the gym, "I need a spot over here. Can you come give me a hand?"

"Wait here, Diane. I'll be right back," the coach said.

"Okay."

Diane leaned on her knees, dropping her head down for more air. This was discouraging. In which part of that split second between up and down should she execute the somersault? She desperately wanted to learn this move. Adrenaline was pumping through her. Just a couple more times and she'd have it. Diane looked up. Apparently the coach was going to be involved for a while, so she decided to do a couple of timers while she was waiting for him to come back.

She took off down the runway, jumped, and pushed off as hard as she could. In the air, her body automatically initiated the somersault, even though her mind was set on doing just a timer. Or was it? Desperately playing catch-up, she over-rotated and came down, smash! The back of her neck thudded into the thick, stiff mat.

Her legs slapped down, and the force of the landing threw her whole body forward into a jet-propelled sit-up. Her face hit her knees. Then her upper torso snapped violently back to the mat, bouncing once before coming to rest. Her eyes wide, Diane lay staring up at the ceiling. Then she felt a shuddering vibration go through her, as if someone was pushing a plunger down through her spine and a coiled spring was unraveling and going out the soles of her feet. She lay there, trying to catch her breath.

Then she tried to sit up. The ceiling beams began to spin, like a giant, rust-red kaleidoscope. Air was seeping out of her like a slow leak in an old, soft balloon, but she couldn't suck it back.

I've hurt myself! The thought was a rude slap in the face. A betrayal. She opened her mouth and a weak, "Help. Somebody help me. I landed on my head" leaked out of her.

Nobody heard. Her life was oozing out onto the floor, and nobody noticed.

In her mind she screamed, but her yell was only a whisper.

Suddenly, the coach was standing over her. Others ran up. They all stood over her with frightened expressions on their white faces. The tour manager, Mike, knelt close to her and said, "We've called an ambulance."

"Are you cold?" someone else asked. Diane didn't answer. She sensed that the others were piling warmup jackets on top of her. Her arms felt heavy.

Somehow, she forced air into her lungs and whispered, "I can't afford to be hurt. My parents don't have much money. Heavenly Father, please help me." All was silent. Tears appeared in her eyes. Then, she felt someone lift her hand. Kurt Thomas knelt beside her. Her fingers curled around his as if they were wet hair.

"You'll be taken care of," a voice behind Kurt said. "Don't worry about the money."

Kurt held her eyes with his. Suddenly, Diane was embarrassed.

"Boy," she whispered, "how many girls would dream of this moment, looking Kurt Thomas right in the eye."

Nervous chuckles erupted. Diane was making jokes, being brave.

Six men in uniforms surrounded her. Someone took an object, a pin? and started poking her. "Can you feel this? That?"

"Yeah. I can feel it."

"Is it sharp or dull?"

"Dull, really dull. It feels like I have socks on." She was breathing better now.

"One, two, three, lift."

Diane tried to lift herself.

"No! No. Don't move! Let us do it."

They strapped her head and body down to the gurney and began rolling her across the gym floor. The rust-red crisscross beams of the ceiling were flying away. She caught a glimpse of the uneven parallel bars and cried out, "I'm so sorry. I hope I didn't ruin the tour. I'm so sorry. I didn't mean to."

Warm moist air of outside hit her face. She saw a red flashing light sweep the air. The sudden terror of being tilted up into the ambulance made her inhale with a gasp. The doors shut. An urgency to talk was upon her.

"Do you think they could turn on the siren so I can tell my little sister? Can we go fast?"

"No, we can't go fast because we don't want to hit any bumps."

"How far away is it?"

"Two minutes."

"That's nice. I've always wanted to ride in an ambulance — my friends will be so impressed . . . "

She went on chattering, as if sound was life itself, when finally, a hand rested on her shoulder. She could feel the strength of it, and the gentleness. She looked up with wet, frightened eyes into a young, handsome face. There was sympathy in his touch and in his voice when he said, "You don't have to keep talking. I know you're scared. You don't have to impress anybody. It's okay."

Is that what she was trying to do? Impress him, others,

herself? Yes, all right. Impress him hard enough to make it true that she was going to be fine!

"Don't worry," she said. "Things always work out for me."

He nodded. She nodded. The fear she had been fighting began to recede. She felt herself being drawn away after it like a rush of fog being sucked into a narrow tunnel. She chased after it, laughing, running, emerging in a burst of clarity to the beginning, where fear had no place.

She was twelve years old again, watching Dad lug that big box into the living room.

"It's a color TV," he boomed as the seven children danced around, excited to the point of hysteria. He leaned over to Diane and said, "We can't watch the Olympics without a color TV, can we?"

Chapter 2

Seeing with impassioned excitement that went deeper than her eyes, Diane watched the 1972 Munich Olympic Games on the new color television set. Olga Korbut, a seventeen-year-old Russian gymnast who was performing on the uneven parallel bars, flew around into her dismount with precisioned impudence. It was almost as if she were stamping her own approval of the performance into the mat, throwing her arms wide to gather the cannonading applause of the audience to her bosom. Then Olga turned full into the camera, and her eyes seemed to go directly to Diane's: "This could be you!"

Diane ran outside to the back lawn and threw herself headlong into a cartwheel. Then another, and another. Six in a row!

Wayne Ellingson saw the fire catch hold in his daughter. He stood in the patio doorway, smiling. There was a spiritual interlinking between them, inexplicable, yet as real as the taste of salt.

"Dad, did you see me?" Diane yelled.

"That's good," he said. "Do some more."

She abruptly threw herself into a full back bend. He leaped to support her around the waist, but with her natural agility she was way ahead of him. "Don't help me!" she commanded. "Let me come back up on my own."

"Sure," he said, as her youthful form snaked up into a standing position.

"You have incredible balance," he said. "Can you do a handstand? No, not like that. You have to keep your chin up, your face looking at your hands. Arch your legs back over your head. No. Here, let me show you."

Show me? thought Diane. She flopped to the grass on her back and looked up right into her dad's face, smiling at her from a perfect handstand beside her.

"I didn't know you could do that!" she screamed.

He laughed, walking away on his hands. "Dad!" she yelled. He crumpled into a heap of laughter, while she piled on to kiss his red, bloated face.

"Let me breathe, let me breathe," he gasped. "I'm too old for this."

"Where did you learn that?" Diane demanded. "Why didn't you ever show me?"

"You never asked me to."

"Oh, Dad."

"I used to be able to do one-handed handstands on a sprinkler head."

"Do it. Do it, now."

"You'll just have to believe me on this one," he grinned. "I don't think the sprinkler could take the forty extra pounds your mom has put on me."

"Oh, Dad."

"Oh, Diane," he mocked. "Come on now, try it my way. Up, and . . . legs way over. You're doing it. Keep your chin forward! Don't fling your legs around like that!"

Diane learned to walk on her hands that afternoon. She felt something rare inside her. A gift. Like someone had given her a glittering diamond. What was she to do with it? "Dad, Mom, I want to be a gymnast," she told her parents that night at supper. "I mean, a real gymnast. I want to go to the Olympics."

Wayne and Gloria Ellingson looked at one another. There was no money for gymnastics lessons. They had seven children, two of whom they were supporting as missionaries in France and Italy. Wayne made a good living as an IBM technician, but with Gloria staying home to care for the children, there simply was not money for gymnastics lessons.

When Wayne reminded her of that, the pain in Diane's eyes only reflected his own.

Diane ran to her bedroom. "It's so unfair!" she wailed, dropping to her knees beside her bed. "Please, please let me be a gymnast," she prayed.

"Diane?" Her mother stood in the doorway. "Honey, what would you have the Lord do?"

"I don't know. Send a box of money to our house . . . I don't know."

"It doesn't work that way, sweetie. Miracles happen, but usually in such small, ordinary ways that people don't recognize them. You have to do all you can yourself, and then, after you've proved your faith, bit by bit, the miracle comes."

The next day she gave Diane a thin book about basic gymnastics. Diane thanked her for it but threw the book against the wall as soon as her mother left the room. Finally, when her anger had subsided to curiosity, she picked it up. Like the sun filtering through a fog, the book, page by page, began to warm Diane's hope. She could do some of this stuff already. She could probably teach herself the rest!

Once that book was exhausted, others from the library followed. Diane spent much of her seventh-grade year teaching herself the skills illustrated in those books.

In eighth grade, she went to the gym teacher and asked if she could join the school gymnastics class. Miss Empey, who often had to scold Diane for showing off during gym class, knew Diane had ability.

"Well, Diane, most of the girls in the class have had a lot more gymnastics training than you."

"I can learn anything."

"I'll tell you what. You can work out with the class after school."

It was the small start of a miracle. Diane gained balance and strength and learned the rules and structure of the sport. She had a taste for all four women's gymnastics events — vaulting horse, balance beam, uneven parallel bars, and floor exercise. At the end of the year, at a district school meet, she placed sixth on bars and seventh in vaulting. In ninth grade she taught herself the advanced-level routines.

The last day of school before Christmas vacation in 1974, Diane was trying to learn a round-off back handspring and hadn't noticed that the rest of the class had assembled over in the corner of the gym.

"Diane, come over here," Miss Empey called. The girls twittered. Diane was usually in a world of her own in class.

"Girls, this is Mrs. Pond." Miss Empey introduced them

to a pert, smiling woman who told them about a gymnastics academy that she and her husband were opening up the street. Diane listened with longing in her heart. How she wished for formal coaching.

After the class ended, Miss Empey said, "Diane, I told her about you. I told her how much talent you have."

"Thank you."

"I also mentioned that you come from a big family and can't afford lessons."

"And she said, 'Forget it,' right?" pouted Diane.

"Wrong, Miss Know-It-All. She said to send you over after the holidays, and they'd see what they could do. Maybe you can earn the lessons. Think about it."

"I will!"

On the fifth of January, Diane took a deep breath, said a little prayer, and entered the gymnastics academy.

"Hi, my name is Diane Ellingson. Miss Empey, my teacher, talked to you about gymnastics lessons."

"Oh, hello. Come with me."

Mrs. Pond led the way to a small room where boxes and odd bits of equipment were strewn every which way. Sitting on a rolled-up mat was an attractive, slender woman with long, strawberry-blonde hair. She wore a T-shirt and jeans.

"Michelle, this is Diane Ellingson, the girl I was telling you about."

"Sit down," said the younger woman without looking up. Diane found a place to sit.

"I'm told you want to be a gymnast."

"Yes, ma'am," said Diane, shyly. "More than anything else in the whole world."

"Why?"

"I want to be just like Olga Korbut. I know I can do it, but . . . I don't have any money to pay for lessons." The woman said nothing, and Diane panicked. "I would do anything in the whole world if you'll just teach me!"

Diane felt foolish. She had actually begged.

"Do you know how to sweep and mop floors?" the woman asked.

"Yes!" Diane blurted, her prospects suddenly opening up.

"Can you wash sinks and scrub toilets?"

"I'll do anything if you'll teach me to be a gymnast."

The woman dropped her head to the side, looking long and hard at Diane. Finally she said, "Well, let's get started. We have a long way to go."

Diane wanted to scream, jump around, cry—she didn't know what, but she didn't dare do anything except follow this icon of pure benevolence named Michelle. Michelle the Magnificent! At that instant, Diane gave Michelle her utmost allegiance, adoration, and loyalty. In return Michelle would give Diane gymnastics—and a kind of immortality.

The gymnasium was brightly lit. New red, white, and blue landing mats lay beneath four sets of smooth, blond wood, uneven parallel bars. At the far end of the room were a trampoline and a vaulting horse. The rest of the room was filled with men's equipment, a horizontal high bar, low parallel bars, and a pommel horse. Diane thought that the new mats had the smell of Christmas dolls. She stood in awe, wondering if heaven itself could be more glorious.

"This is the downstairs gym. There's more upstairs."

More? Upstairs, Diane stood speechless. Another trampoline. Two trampolines! Another vaulting horse, and rings, and a high bar with a thick crash mat underneath. On the stage along one side were four balance beams, and at the far end of the room were two more. Filling the rest of the room was the most beautiful blue plush carpet floor-exercise mat Diane had ever seen. She had only worked out on rubber wrestling mats. Truly, this had to be a dream. The rest of the evening was pure ecstasy.

Charlie Pond introduced himself. He was a robust man of about sixty with flowing white hair stuffed up under a Russian peasant hat. He told Diane about the Utah Academy of Gymnastics. Diane was awestruck to learn that he had been coach to several Olympians and national champions, two of whom would be coaching this club—his own daughter, Michelle, and a young man named Paul Hunt.

Charlie launched into a detailed explanation of the safety rules in the gym. He showed her an invention of his called a traveling spotting belt with a twisting mechanism that allowed total movement but kept the gymnast from crashing to the floor. "Would you like to try it out?" he asked. Diane flew to her feet. "Do you know how to do a back handspring? No? Good. We call it a 'flic-flac' here."

With complete faith in these strangers whom she had already embraced as her mentors, Diane leaped backwards into the air. Each time she did, the ropes attached to the spotting belt suspended her up and over. After just a few tries, she did it herself without the belt. "Be here right at 3:30 tomorrow for class," said Michelle when the evening was over.

A grueling three-hour workout greeted Diane the next day, including calisthenics as well as gymnastics and equipment training. When it was over, the other kids in the Academy dragged themselves out to parents waiting to drive them home, but Diane hobbled to the utility closet and emerged with a bucket and mop in hand.

"Where do you want me to start?" she asked Michelle

"The floor's okay. If you see blood on the equipment, wipe it off."

An hour later, her own blistered hands still oozing blood, Diane walked the three blocks home. She dragged herself past the dinner table, up the stairs, and into bed. She lay there unable to move, unable to change into her pajamas, unable to stop the tears that squeezed out from between her tightly shut eyelids. They trickled down her face into her ears and soaked the hair at the back of her neck.

"Why are you crying, honey?" her mother asked as she came into the room. She sat on the bed, gently smoothing the hair back off Diane's face.

"I'm not crying. I'm happy, so happy . . . "

Diane fell deeply asleep as her mother undressed her, put Vaseline on her torn palms, and wrapped her hands in a towel. She tucked the bed covers up under her daughter's chin and then left the room but returned a few moments later to place a brand-new, pink leotard at the foot of Diane's bed. She turned out the light and went downstairs to warn Marie, Louise, and Laura not to wake up Diane when they went to bed.

The next afternoon, near the end of the three-hour work-out, Charlie produced a video camera and taped every girl doing a floor routine. Diane wore her new pink leotard and yellow ankle socks.

"You look like an ostrich!" yelled one of the little girls when Diane popped up on the television screen. It was true. Diane was only four feet eleven and weighed eighty pounds, but she looked tall and skinny compared to the other girls. She was fourteen years old, an age when many gymnasts were already well into their careers. She blushed as pink as her leotard when she saw herself on the screen. "I look kind of awkward, don't I?" she asked.

"You don't look like an ostrich, but you do look like a bird," said Michelle, "a bird who's learning to fly."

Diane made a friend, a twelve-year-old named Shannon, who was the best gymnast in the club. In the next three months, Diane pushed herself to match Shannon's skill. Diane was years behind and couldn't stand it. She learned as many as four or five skills on some days, especially on the uneven parallel bars, the event she seemed made for. She was sure that this game of catch-up was taking too long, failing to understand that while she was learning five skills a day, the others were doing well to learn one. And no matter how the day went in the gym, good or bad, she always had the mop and broom to tell her story to.

Six months after she started with the Academy, Paul videotaped their routines again. This time, Diane performed an entire beam routine she had been working on for a week, including a back handspring on the high beam, for the first time without a spotter. The high beam stands four feet off the ground and the beam itself is a wooden rail only four inches wide, which leaves a very narrow margin for error. Diane didn't fall, though. When playing the tape back, Paul picked at the mistakes in her routine, but Diane wasn't listening. She saw before her on the television screen not an ugly ostrich but a beautiful, graceful gymnast. Paul was talking about the little flaws an artist picks out while sculpting perfection, but Diane was thrilled and said just loud enough for a few to hear, "I look like a beautiful bird."

"I told you you'd learn to fly," said Michelle. "We'll have to call you 'Bird' from now on. 'Big Bird.' That's good. 'Big Bird.' "

Chapter 3

"Hey, Big Bird," Michelle laughed. "Are your parents home?"

Diane was dazed. It was strange seeing Paul and Michelle anywhere but in the gym. Then, seeing her parents greet the two of them as they would greet anyone else was even more strange. Diane thought her coaches should be treated as if they were royalty.

"Mr. and Mrs. Ellingson, we want to talk to you about Diane."

Why? thought Diane. She had been trying really hard, and she was never late.

"Sweetheart," said Diane's dad, "why don't you go on out of here for a few minutes and leave us alone."

Diane shuffled noisily down the hall and then sneaked quietly back to hide just around the corner.

"Diane has an exceptional gift," she heard Michelle say. "We think she could really go somewhere with this, and we want to step up her training from three days a week to seven."

"Well . . . ," began her father, but he was cut off by Diane's leaping back into the room and onto his lap, screaming, "Please, please, please!"

"Hey, now, young lady," he said, firmly planting Diane back on the floor, "you just let me talk. First of all, we won't even consider training or competing on Sunday. Diane goes to church on Sunday, and on Tuesday night she goes to her church youth meeting. Besides that, we want her with us Monday for family home evening and on vacations during the summer."

"All right," said Michelle.

"Hot dog!" yelled Diane.

Paul said, "You can forget scrubbing the toilets from now on, too, Diane. You won't have time for that anymore. You can earn your keep by being a junior leader with the little ones. Okay?"

"Okay!"

Diane trained six days a week for the rest of the summer. During the school year she received tenth-grade physical education credit from the high school, which allowed her to leave for the Academy after fifth period. Her dad picked her up most nights on his way home from work. If he arrived early, he stayed to watch. It was impossible for him to account for the pride he felt in his daughter. One day he started calling her "Big D."

Diane's friendship with Shannon solidified, the center of their relationship being gymnastics. While Diane's other friends in high school were discussing boys and clothes, Diane and Shannon discussed nothing but gymnastics. They both wore their hair pulled back in ponytails, out of the way, and neither bothered with much makeup. One of the girls in the gym had a boyfriend. He hung around near the end of workout, distracting her, constantly urging her to cut out early or call in sick. That girl was a second-rate gymnast. Diane and Shannon equated boys with mediocrity.

The only male Diane trusted, other than her father, was Paul. She had a terrible crush on him. When she did something particularly well, he would say, "Good girl, Diane," and it made her giddy.

Paul and Michelle were opposites. She was fair and willowy, unusually tall for a woman gymnast. Paul was short, powerfully stocky, and dark. Both coaches could, and did, yell a lot. Yelling was part of the coaching atmosphere of the gym. A very regimented, demanding discipline was maintained most of the time, yet with their different personalities, Paul and Michelle counterbalanced one another's coaching style.

Paul taught with patience and humor, moving from one girl to the other, spotting, adjusting equipment, being with but staying aloof from them. Sometimes he launched into mimicry of the wrong moves the students made on the beam. Of course, deliberately doing the wrong moves took tremendous coordination and exacting skill. Occasionally he cavorted on and on, the kids laughing until their sides ached. He bounced about on the floor, flapping his hands, stumbling on tiptoe on the beam, his face pulled into idiotic bewilderment. His mustache made him look all the more ludicrous. With incredible strength, he pulled himself up into a handstand on the balance beam, floundering in every direction. His legs crossed around the beam, he slipped underneath it, still hanging on by his knees. Pressing his hands together in an attitude of prayer, he batted his eyelashes and wailed, "Please, oh please, get me down from here, Michelle."

Michelle always rolled her eyes in disgust.

Michelle coached with humorless intensity, lecturing from her perch on the stage, yet her involvement was pointedly personal. If there were problems, Paul would say to her, "I don't want to have anything to do with this," and walk away. Michelle never walked away. She drove her will into the heart of every student, accepted no compromise, and became irate when her point of view was questioned. By her very intensity, she won Diane's complete devotion. She drew the best from Diane, and Diane returned absolute love.

In September, Paul and Michelle took Diane and Shannon to the World Games Trials in California. At one time during the all-night drive of fourteen hours, Diane sat in the front seat next to Michelle. Michelle talked to Diane just as she would talk to a friend, asking her opinion on various unremarkable subjects, being at ease, even laughing at Diane's elephant jokes. When the long night wore away the desire to talk, Diane snuggled back against the door and sat staring at her idol. Finally, Michelle looked over and smiled.

"Why don't you go to sleep, hon?" Michelle asked.

"No, I want to keep you company."

Paul and Michelle had taken Diane and Shannon to the World Games Trials to expose them to serious, competitive gymnastics. The meet was thrilling to Diane. She sat within feet of gymnasts of the caliber of Olga Korbut. She shook hands with Nancy Theis, one of Charlie's former students who had been in the 1972 Olympics with Olga. Diane wanted to be one of the greats. She couldn't get back home to the Academy fast enough. She would train even harder. So much time had been lost. Nancy Theis was younger than Diane was now when she went to the Olympics.

The spark had been fanned, and Diane was fully on fire. Michelle was a master at the forge. She hammered away, and Diane malleably accepted the blows.

Diane learned quickly that sympathy was a rare commodity in the real world of serious gymnastics. She picked up the habit very early of keeping her mouth shut about aches and pains. Crying was not tolerated in the gym. After a few minutes of rest, she would be back at workout, and eventually, the pain was shoved to the back of her mind where it became an habitual vagrant.

Diane took to the bars like a bird to the loftiest air currents. She was a natural. With ballet training added to the regimen, her floor exercise strengthened, but mastering the vaulting horse, and especially the beam, became the trial of her talents. Those didn't come easy. She had to work as hard at not becoming discouraged as she worked at learning the skills themselves.

"Diane, you're sweating like a pig!" yelled Shannon one day from over by the mats.

"Mind your own business, smarty-pants!" Paul yelled back at her. Diane had been doing back handsprings on the beam, a skill she had learned but which was still shaky. Suddenly, sweat ran from her hairline into her eyes, and when she tried to wipe it out with her forearm, she lost her balance and fell. Her inner thigh slammed against the beam. As hard as she fought them, tears mingled with the perspiration running down her face.

"Are you injured?" Michelle called out from her place on the stage.

"No," said Diane, but the pain in her voice came out as a whine.

"Get back up and do it again, and then you can go take care of your leg," Michelle said.

Diane climbed up but then stood frozen with fear. She took a few breaths, wiped her sweaty hands on her thighs, and posed, only to hesitate and stop again.

Paul said, "Go ahead. I'm right here."

She put her arms out once more, wiggled her fingers, but couldn't make herself do it.

"I'll spot you on one, then you have to do it by yourself," Paul said. Michelle watched like a hawk.

With Paul's strong hands behind her back, Diane did it. "Now, do it without me," Paul said.

Diane gave Paul a pleading look. Finally, Michelle said, "Diane, either do it or go home."

The ultimate threat. Diane closed her eyes, swallowed, held her breath, flew back into an arch, and grabbed the beam with her hands. Then she pulled her legs up and over. She caught the beam with one foot, but she pushed quickly away so that she wouldn't straddle it and fell to the floor.

"All right, that's a start," snapped Michelle with a sharp clap of her hands, obviously pleased. "Now try it again."

This time, Diane caught the beam with both feet. It wasn't very pretty, but she did it, and Michelle nodded and said, "Now you can go get some ice on that leg."

Diane went downstairs. The bruise was already enormous and swollen. She held a paper cup filled with ice to her leg and allowed a few tears to fall when no one could see.

"I did it!" she whispered to herself. "Michelle knew I could do it."

That year both Diane, in the senior division, and Shannon, in the junior division, took first place all-around in the

Utah State Class-1 Qualifying Meet. They then went on to win the all-around in the state meet in their divisions. Regionals were held that year in Salt Lake City. Shannon qualified for junior nationals, to be held in Washington, D.C. Diane qualified for senior nationals, to be held in Eugene, Oregon.

Considering that this was the Academy's first full year and Diane's first year of national-level competition, her performance was phenomenal. Her name began floating around the Utah gymnastics circuit as something of a wonder kid from the new club. When Nancy Theis came to Utah to do a statewide gymnastics clinic, Diane and Shannon afterward performed their routines in their own gym for Nancy, eagerly accepting her criticisms and suggestions as well as a good deal of honest praise. She regaled them with accounts of glory and the thrill of being in the Olympics.

"What advice would you give these two girls, Nancy?" Michelle asked.

Nancy was barely older than Diane herself. She said, "You love gymnastics right now. Your life is gymnastics, and you can't imagine that you would ever get discouraged or feel like giving up. But you will. You're going to try things, and you're going to fall. You're going to compete, and you're not going to win. Everybody falls and everybody loses sometimes in gymnastics."

Diane listened but didn't believe. Nancy saw the look in Diane's face, recognizing the naivete of her ambition.

"It's true. You'll lose a lot more than you'll win. You'll fall a lot more than you'll stick. Just remember, if you fall down and stay down, you're a quitter and a loser and you'll never win. If you get back up every time you fall and you try once more, eventually it will be your turn to be a champion."

Diane had heard all that before, but it had never touched her. Sitting before her was a true champion, someone who knew what it was like to hold the bouquet of roses. But what was all this about falling and losing? It wasn't what Diane wanted to hear. Surely it would be different for her.

"Set your goals as high as the stars," Nancy was saying. "You see, if you reach for the stars, you might get lucky and peak the mountain. If you reach for the mountain, you might peak the housetops. But, if you only reach for the house-tops . . . "

They all laughed. "Right, you'll barely get off the ground."

The next day at workout, Michelle said to Diane, "Nancy was really impressed with your bars."

"What did she say?"

"She says your routine is as good as any she's seen in the whole country."

"Hot dog! What else did she say?"

"She can't believe you've taken lessons for only a year. She doesn't think it's unrealistic for you and Shannon to try for Elite this year. You'll have to learn the Elite compulsories and go to some Elite clinics in California."

"Oh, rats!" Diane grinned.

"It's going to take a lot of work, though. You better believe it."

Of the many levels of amateur gymnastics, Elite, or Olympic level, is the highest. Diane and Shannon jumped straight for Elite. Paul and Michelle decided to enter the two in the AAU Senior Nationals held in Cedar Rapids, Iowa. This Elite meet was the competition just under Olympic trials, World

Games trials, and the USA championships, yet no qualifying scores were needed to participate.

Diane felt out of place in that meet, like a kid watching the greats perform inside the family color television set — only now, she was in there with them. Her rise in gymnastics had been so meteoric that she hadn't had time to tack the image of champion to herself.

The first day was compulsory routines; the second, optionals. Even though she knew she wasn't the best, Diane was thrilled with her performance, especially on bars. She had never expected to win, even though a glimmer of hope for a miracle fired her, as it does every competitor. The two days were filled with excitement. The atmosphere alone made her feel as if she was living on pure adrenaline. She marveled to realize that only hundredths of points separated her from famous gymnasts, and sometimes, that same margin put her ahead of them. She was no longer a novice.

Michelle slipped onto the bench next to her. "Diane, it looks like you made finals on bars."

"What?" Diane would have leaped to her feet, but Michelle already had her in a bear hug. "Now don't get excited," Michelle laughed.

Oh, sure, thought Diane.

"The final scores aren't in yet. You have to make the top eight to be in the finals, but you're looking awfully good, hon."

When the unofficial first tally of scores came out, though, Diane was in ninth place. Try as she might, it was impossible for Diane to hide the disappointment she felt. To have come so close! Tears were fighting to the surface, but she blinked them back when Nancy Theis walked up.

"Diane, I'll scratch bars in finals so you can compete if you'd like to," Nancy said.

"Huh?"

Nancy smiled. "If I scratch, you'll move into eighth place, and you can compete."

"You'd do that for me?" Diane's head was spinning. Nancy was an Olympian. Everybody knew her. "How can you give up a chance for a medal so I can compete? There's probably no way I'll place for a medal."

"I want you to have the chance anyway," Nancy said, squeezing Diane's hand.

As it turned out, when the final scores came blasting out of the loud speaker, Diane was in eighth place after all. Nancy had not had to make the sacrifice.

Diane drew her number that evening. She would compete sixth; Nancy was fifth. Diane watched the other gymnasts and then said a prayer as Nancy chalked her hands, set the bars, and stood motionless, pulling herself together for her routine.

Nancy's mount was perfect. She jumped off the springboard and stretched into a half-twist, long-hang kip on the high bar. Diane's throat caught at the grace, the sheer perfection of it. She wanted Nancy to win. She had never prayed for anyone else so hard before.

. . . beat the low bar . . . full twist . . . beat . . .

Then the impossible happened. At the end of a sole circle one-and-a-half twist, Nancy reached for and missed the high bar. She missed it — and fell off the bars! Diane couldn't believe it. Nancy jumped back up, finished the routine, and then walked off the floor with a smile on her face.

Diane was sick. She wanted to go to Nancy and cry with her, knowing how disappointed she must be, but there wasn't time. Diane was up next. She chalked her hands and then set the guy-wire tension on the bars for maximum flexibility. She ran and jumped. The bar was responsive, submissive, playful. Diane forgot where she was. Suddenly, nothing was important but to have fun, and it was such fun. She felt she was flying — soaring and bouncing through a cloud of laughter. She landed the dismount, waved, and walked off the floor.

The competition ended, they called out the first four winners' names, and then they called Diane's. Awash with ecstasy, she stood on the victory stand in fifth place, while Nancy Theis and other Olympians sat on the sidelines cheering.

Nancy engulfed Diane as soon as she stepped off the stand. "Diane, I am so proud of you. You keep reaching for the stars and you're going to make it big. I just know it."

A few weeks before, Diane had begun keeping a journal. It was already one of her treasures. She felt that writing kept all the miracles that had happened to her from dying, the essence of wonder clinging to the pages like precious perfume. That night she opened to a blank page and wrote the details of the day's events. Then she stopped, unable to find just the right words to express her feelings about the momentous lessons she had learned. Finally, she shrugged and scribbled, frustrated with the only way she knew how to say it:

"Champions fall, too. Can you believe it?"

Chapter 4

"Make those wings touch, angel," Charlie laughed. "That's the stuff."

Charlie, this time wearing a New York Yankee baseball cap, came up behind Diane and moulded her shoulders back and straight, just as he had done almost every day in the first six months she was at the Academy. "Be proud of yourself. Show it!" he said, smiling as broadly as ever. Diane smiled back and pinched her shoulder blades together as tight as she could force them.

As soon as he rounded the stairwell and bounded down out of sight, she relaxed, but only a little. She felt like looking proud. Standing on the victory stand at AAU Senior Nationals had put happiness in her marrow. She carried energized confidence in her gait.

"Hey, Diane, numero cinco!" screeched Shannon when Diane walked into the gym. Shannon and several of the younger girls came running and pounced. Diane could barely hold her balance during the barrage of excited hugs.

"You did us proud," said Shannon. "You were the best!"

"Don't get cocky," laughed Michelle from over on her perch. "You've only got two weeks to train for Class I nationals. Get stretched out and warm up. We're starting on bars today!"

Diane put on her hand grips, chalked up, and with a whoop of delight, jumped up to the bars and started flying. Three long hang kips, beat, back up, rise to a straight body, free-hip circle, handstand, beat the bars, front somersault, half turn, drop glide kip, catch, straddle over, kip to the high bar, cast hecht dismount. Stick!

Michelle yelled, "Diane, I said warm up, not show off. Doing a bar routine cold is a good way to get yourself hurt."

Diane grabbed a towel and buried her face in it, trying to wipe her smile off. Then, mopping the sweat from her forehead, she called, "I'm always warmed up on bars. I could stick a bar routine in my sleep!"

Paul sauntered over. The other girls were busy getting their grips on, chalking their hands, and setting the bars.

"You have to stick six optionals before you can go on today."

The usual chorus of groans greeted this news.

"Hey, you get to stay on bars until you do it. I don't care if it takes all night." He turned to Diane. "Since you're already so hot, you can get back up there and keep going."

The third time through her routine, while gripping the chalky bar on top in a straight-arm handstand, one of Diane's leather handgrips shifted ever so slightly. When she dropped around in a free-hip circle, a wart that had been growing below her thumb ripped off.

"What a spaz!" Diane yelled, dropping to her feet on the mat. Blood gushed from the hole in her hand, soaking into the gray leather protection pad of her hand grip. She ripped the buckle open with her teeth and spat the bloody thing to the mat, while she jammed the thumb of her other hand into the wound. "Ow, ow, ow," she danced as the blood flowed into her palm.

She ran to the chalk bucket and forced the dry powder into the hole in her hand. It didn't work. Bleeding blisters actually felt better when you crammed chalk into them, but this wart was something different. No matter how much chalk she used, the wound just wouldn't stop bleeding, nor would it numb. It hurt like crazy.

"What a spaz," she chanted over and over. Michelle handed her a towel and said, "For heaven's sake, Diane, go put some ice on it."

"Way to get out of bar routines," yelled Shannon as Diane left the gym.

"How would you like to do the rest of hers, Shannon?" yelled Michelle. "I don't like your attitude!"

Shannon set her teeth.

"And you can write a report tonight, Shannon," Michelle yelled. "Five pages on the value of workout!"

Michelle was always having them write reports when she was peeved. Most of the girls hated reports, but Diane found them a way to communicate her feelings when talking wouldn't do it. Diane ran down the stairs to the bathroom. It took a long time for the wound to stop bleeding, and it stung like fire.

When Diane walked back into the gym, Paul called her over. A chunk of callus was hanging from Diane's palm.

"This looks like hamburger," said Diane, hoping for a little sympathy.

"You're right. It looks terrible this way," said Paul. He suddenly grabbed her hand and quickly pulled the loose callus the rest of the way off. "Now, that looks a lot better. You're up next. You've got three more routines to go."

Tears fought to the surface, but Diane relentlessly forced them back. She remembered one of the first things Shannon had said to her when she joined the Academy: "If you're fixin' to start boobin,' you can forget it. There's no mercy in this gym."

By this time, all the other girls had finished their routines and had gone with Michelle to work beam. Diane was left to Paul. She got another set of handgrips, chalked up extra heavy, and climbed back up on the bars, forcing back into the recesses of dead thought her consciousness of raw flesh rubbing into stiff leather. She became a machine with eyes glazed over and teeth set. When bar work was over, she went on to beam, vault, and finally to ballet training.

"Lift your heads," the ballet master chanted as both boys and girls were put through nearly an hour of ballet rigor.

"Drop your shoulders, soften your arms."

Usually ballet was fun, but today it was just plain painful. Diane had forgotten her sore hand because now every movement was torture to her legs.

"How ya doin,' Dine?" asked Shannon.

"Okay, Shan."

Actually, Diane was worried. Her ankles were hurting badly and during vault training, they had felt like they were crumbling. Her shins were burning, but there was no way she was going to complain. Not anymore today.

"Throw your chest out! Perform for the last row in the balcony!"

Diane reasoned that if she kept silent, the pain in her ankles would probably go away.

It didn't. At home, Diane lay on the sofa with her legs in her mother's lap. She rubbed them while she read to the smaller children. Later, Diane fell asleep in bed while her mom iced her ankles. At school the next day, she could barely walk. Finally, Diane went to Michelle.

"My ankles hurt. I don't know what's the matter with them."

"Show me."

"Right inside the bones. They're burning."

Paul had seen the two of them move to the sideline and came to investigate.

"What's the matter, Diane?" he asked.

"Something's wrong with my ankles."

"You've got nationals in two weeks. You don't have time to be hurt."

Diane looked at him with wide eyes.

"I think it's all in your head!" he barked, but Diane's look made him add, a little more kindly, "These things happen sometimes after a big success. All of a sudden you have something to live up to and subconsciously it freaks you out."

By now, Charlie had joined the little huddle. He chimed in his agreement with Paul that it was probably all in her head. She clamped her mouth shut and finished out the day trying to ignore the agony that wasn't supposed to be there.

The next day at workout she suddenly cried out in the middle of tumbling. Paul was spotting.

"I don't want to hear it. Suffer in silence," he growled.

Diane looked over at Michelle on the stage, but she had her face buried in the code of points book, the gymnastics bible. Diane set her teeth to keep the tears from forming. The next day, however, her mother took her to a doctor, who said she had tendonitis. He prescribed Butazolidin, an antiinflammatory agent widely used by gymnasts at the time, and he shot cortisone into her ankles. "This will numb it up for you anyway," he said. Diane told Charlie the diagnosis the next day in the gym.

"That's what they always say when they can't find anything wrong," he said. "I think it's all in your head."

Diane got through the next few days of workout feeling so much better that she left for nationals without going back to the doctor for another treatment. The first day of compulsories wasn't bad. The next day, though, she woke with pain in her ankles. It increased during warmup. She slipped over to the water cooler and took four extra-strength aspirin tablets. They hit her stomach like electric shocks, but after a while the pain dimmed. Paul, who was watching, asked if she'd be all right. Diane nodded. He gave her a little hug.

"Thatta girl," he said. "Let me tape those ankles for you."

Bars were Diane's specialty, but as hard as she tried, she couldn't get enough power off the springboard to do the somersault mount over the low bar and missed the high bar. She landed on one foot on the floor. Pulling herself back up onto the bars, she finished her routine, landing the dismount again on one foot.

Beam was disaster. She fell twice and tumbled out of the dismount landing. Still, neither Paul nor Michelle showed sympathy.

That night in bed, Diane was consumed with loneliness.

Believing her coaches thought she was a faker hurt even more than realizing she'd made a miserable failure of herself at nationals. Now she could cry, now when there wasn't an audience to see her. Everything she had worked so hard for seemed to fade out of her reach all at once.

The next day, when she arrived home, her mother took her back to the doctor. "You've got to lay off," he insisted. "We need to cast your ankles—at least the right one."

A mixture of fear and relief came over Diane. "Okay, but I have to talk to my coaches first," she said.

"Your coaches will decide if we cast it?"

"Yes."

Michelle and Paul reacted to the news much as Diane expected.

"This is great," said Michelle. "You can't afford to be injured. You can't afford to take time off."

Paul said, "You're going to miss this whole summer of training, now," his frustration translating as disgust in Diane's ears. "But that doesn't mean you won't be at the gym. There will be plenty you can do."

That summer, Diane spent five hours a day, six days a week, training with the team and another three to four hours until 9:00 P.M. with her class of novices as well.

Even with the cast on her leg, she learned bits and pieces of an entire new set of routines. At first, it was just calisthenics. Then she started working handstands on the beam, eventually coercing Paul to spot her through tricks, even killers on bars. She actually performed her dismount, a hecht off the high bar, with Paul catching the landing so she wouldn't break the cast.

Still, her training suffered. Unable to run, dance, and

tumble, having only one fairly good leg, her work on the floor, beam, and vaulting horse suffered most. Still, by the fall of her junior year, she qualified for Elite nationals, and in February 1976 she, Shannon, and a third girl named Jackie, along with Michelle, boarded an airplane bound for Minneapolis. Qualifying at Elite nationals would officially make her an Elite, or Olympic level, gymnast. Traveling with Michelle was usually strictly business. Rent a car, look at the gym, go to the hotel, go to bed. That's how it was. But this time, they went sight-seeing and afterward to dinner. Diane couldn't figure out what had gotten into Michelle. She was positively jovial. They ate spaghetti and then went back to the room they all four shared.

In the morning Michelle did their hair. Diane's was pulled back in a ponytail with three tight curls in it and then sprayed so heavily with hair spray that it felt like a stiff bread dough sculpture. It had to be lacquered down to survive the flip-flopping during the meet. Then there was a frustrating four-hour delay the first morning while the coaches and officials met to argue over the rules. Finally, the meet was underway.

After Diane's two tries at the compulsory vault, Michelle complained, "You're still pushing off too late, Diane. You don't open the pike quick enough."

Her beam routine was excellent until the end, when she suddenly got shaky. On bars, she was her usual dazzling self, but her floor routine reflected the summer months of laying off.

"It stunk," Diane said to Shannon as she walked off the floor. Earlier in the meet a girl from another club who had done poorly stomped off the floor in a temper tantrum. Michelle turned to her girls and said, "If I ever see you pull a stunt like that, I'll never take you to another meet." So now, even though Diane felt like kicking somebody, she smiled a huge, theatrical "Michelle smile," her face nearly breaking in half with the effort.

After that first day, Michelle called all the girls to the corner of the back stairwell. She sat a few stairs up while they sat on the floor.

"Jackie, you looked stiff as a board out there, and Diane, you didn't finish one dance move on floor. You looked like you were doing everything halfway."

People walked past them on the stairs, and even though they had to dodge around her to get by, Michelle didn't seem to notice them. She just kept drilling while the girls ducked in embarrassment.

"I don't know what you were doing out there. You didn't apply one thing we've been working on for the last three weeks. None of you have. You better shape up tomorrow!"

The girls ate spaghetti again that night, but with Michelle's anger sitting like a volcano in their stomachs, it didn't taste as good. "Blame the equipment or make excuses in front of Michelle, and you're fixin' for trouble," grumbled Shannon to Diane in the elevator.

Diane was frozen with nervousness the next day during warm-ups for optionals. She wanted so much to make Elite. It was her life's obsession. She wished for it on every first star at night and whenever she went through a yellow light in a car or over railroad tracks. She thought about it constantly and prayed for it every night. Now, because she wanted it so badly, the tension in her body was paralyzing. A thought flashed through her mind — something Michelle had told her a month earlier. "To be an Elite gymnast, you have to act like an Elite gymnast." Diane started breathing more slowly, and her throat began working again.

During competition she fell off the beam once. One-half point was taken off for that, but still she was happy because the rest of her routine felt solid, and she stuck it. With her vault it was hard to tell. It seemed pretty good.

On the other hand, Diane just couldn't quite make up for the bad summer, a late start, and lost experience. Her bars and floor routine suffered. Before the final scores were announced, Diane and Michelle made some hasty calculations on the back of a paper bag and came up showing Diane only fifteen-hundredths of a point from making Elite.

"Oh, it isn't enough, Bird," Michelle said.

Diane wanted to die. Only .15 away from the portal to her fondest dream. Those few shaky steps, that one fall, had dragged her backwards just enough to keep her outside while the door slammed shut in her face. Michelle was busy calculating on the paper, rechecking the figures. She said, "But, there's one more thing we can try. Your bar score could have been a little low. They might raise that."

Michelle walked away to protest Diane's bar score. In the meantime, Diane sat hunched over, pretending to look for something in her gym bag while she prayed, "Heavenly Father, please let me be an Elite gymnast. I've worked hard. I've given my best. I've tried to do what's right. Please let them raise my score."

Michelle came back. "They wouldn't do it, Diane. They just wouldn't budge. There's nothing else we can do."

Tears welled up in Diane's eyes.

"No tears here, Diane. I know you're disappointed, but I expect you to keep your chin up."

Diane nodded. Michelle gave her shoulders a squeeze. "Thatta girl."

It wasn't until later that night at dinner as she sat listening to Jackie and Shannon, who had both qualified for national Elites in Pennsylvania, that it finally hit her. She wouldn't be going with them. She was not an Elite gymnast. She was no longer in the embrace of Shannon's world.

Diane tried hard to show genuine happiness for Shannon and Jackie, but later, in the darkness of the bedroom, when she was finally convinced that Michelle had fallen asleep, she allowed her misery some rein. She lay there feeling the hot tears coming out of her eyes. It all seemed so unjust.

Then, to her horror, she heard Michelle stir. She pretended to be asleep, but in a kind, almost motherly voice Michelle said, "It's okay to cry. You're not in the gym now. I know how bad you feel."

"It hurts so much," cried Diane.

Michelle pulled her close, speaking softly into the darkness.

"I know."

"It's not that I'm not happy for Shannon and Jackie. I am." Diane hoped Michelle understood.

"I know."

"It's just that I don't get to be a part of them anymore. I feel like I'm on one side of a brick wall, and they're on the other. I almost made it over the top, but somehow I fell off and now I'm back at the very beginning, to start all over again, where I was a year ago."

"No way, not where you were a year ago," soothed Michelle. "Diane, you've come so far in such a short time. You've been unbelievable. Not a kid in a million could have done what you've done. You can try for Elite again next year."

"But the Olympics are this summer. Not qualifying for Elite this year took away all my chances of ever qualifying for the Olympic team."

"I see," said Michelle softly into the heavy sadness of the moment.

The commiseration in Michelle's voice was deeply comforting. Diane realized that Michelle had experienced this same disappointment in her own life years before when she hadn't qualified for the Olympic team.

Diane sobbed into Michelle's bosom for a long time. She could smell Michelle's perfume. Tabu. A scent that would forever trigger one of the dearest affections of her life. Michelle was silent, except for a few soothing hums as she gently patted Diane's back. Finally, Diane whispered.

"I guess I could try for Elite next year."

"Sure you could."

"I can make the best out of being Class I now, though," Diane whispered hopefully into the dark.

"Sure you can," Michelle said.

"I guess it will be just as hard to be the national Class I champion as to make Elite."

"You better believe it," said Michelle. "You'll have to get started right away, so maybe you'd better get to sleep, okay, Big Bird?"

"Okay," said Diane. She loved this mean old coach. She really did.

Chapter 5

Diane's goal of becoming the national Class I champion was a fire, driving her like a steamroller. Her ankles started hurting again three weeks before the state meet, but she didn't say anything to Paul and Michelle. She was sure she could make them hold out with prayer and aspirin, and she did. In spite of the dull burn underneath an aspirin overload, Diane had a good competition at the state meet, but another girl from another club had a better one. Diane slipped once during optional bars, and the other girl hit every event. In the end, Diane took second, now having lost not only Elite but the state Class I title as well.

"But I still qualify for regionals," Diane said to Michelle.

"Diane, your ankles worry me. I know you aren't telling me everything."

"I'll lay off workout for the next two weeks. The legs'll be strong. I want to go so bad. I couldn't stand staying home. Please!"

"Okay. Okay."

Regionals were held in Santa Clara, California. At the end of compulsories the first day, results showed Diane in seventh place, but during optional warmups on floor the next day, her ankles started to throb. They grew worse and worse after each tumbling pass. Finally, Michelle took her to the side.

"Do you want to scratch?"

Diane was mortified.

"No, I don't want to scratch!" she said, and to prove her determination, she ran and flew into a full-twisting somersault. She crash landed, and it was obvious that she didn't prove anything, because Michelle turned and walked away, returning a few minutes later to say, "Paul and I want to talk to you outside."

The three of them crowded into a quiet doorway. Michelle told Diane that they recommended she scratch the meet.

"A few more hard hits on that ankle will put you out for another summer," said Paul. Michelle put her arm around Diane's slumping shoulders.

"Listen," Michelle said, "if you scratch now and let the ankle heal, you could probably be petitioned into the nationals this year with the regionals score you have now."

Diane could tell that Michelle wasn't just bluffing for some little kid who couldn't take the truth.

"Okay, I'll scratch," she said.

That night while traveling home in the van with Paul and Michelle, Diane pulled out her journal. "I can't win," she wrote, completely depressed.

Michelle turned around in her seat. "Diane, you ought to

let me read your journal sometime. I bet it would help me be a better coach to see what you've written."

Diane smiled, but she knew she'd never let Michelle read her journal. I write the way I feel, Diane thought to herself. Michelle wouldn't like me after reading how I really am.

"Well, maybe sometime," Diane said, extremely glad when Michelle didn't push the issue.

That week, Diane consulted with an orthopedic specialist.

"Quit gymnastics," he said.

"I can't quit gymnastics," Diane said, looking at the doctor.

"Why not?"

"I have dreams—I have hopes. Look, you just quit being a doctor! Could you do that? Quit breathing or something, and maybe you'll understand why I can't quit gymnastics. Besides, I have nationals in three weeks."

Diane hobbled to the Academy every day, frantic to keep up with training as best she could. She took it easy, landing everything, even the basic tricks, with a spotter. She put ice treatments on her ankles and downed bottles of extra-strength aspirin.

But still, three weeks wasn't enough time and nationals happened without her. Summer training began. The pressure of competition was off, making Michelle and Paul a lot more relaxed. The weeks were spent learning new routines between a lot of goofing off.

At the end of August, Diane, who was seventeen, went on her first date. At a family reunion in Idaho she met the younger brother of her sister-in-law. Steve was sixteen and a wrestler on his high school team. The two young people were like beautiful animals, sparring, teasing, talking of their re-

spective sports. "Do you want to go bowling?" he asked for
the next evening.

"Sure."

Diane was excited. She had been asked out before but had
always said no because of her time commitment to gymnastics.
Here in Idaho, away from the gym, there was no reason not
to go.

She had heard what to do on dates and knew about the
essential social graces, yet when they pulled up outside the
bowling alley in Steve's car, she reached for the door handle
and cracked open the door. Suddenly she realized the blunder
she had made. Steve was already out of the car and coming
around to open her door for her. She let her hand slip back
into her lap and prayed that he wouldn't notice. He didn't
say anything.

She won two bowling games and let him win two and was
feeling smugly ladylike as he walked her back to the car. Again
old habit prevailed, but this time when she reached out to
open the door he intervened, grinning.

"Aren't you going to let me open it first this time?" he
teased.

Diane turned crimson. What must he think of her?

"And next time, it's okay to let me lose. I'm used to it."

"You must think I'm really dumb."

"Naw. I just won't take you bowling again."

"Really?"

"Just kidding. I'll have to find a sport you aren't better at
than I am. Maybe we could wrestle."

Diane glanced up at this perfectly handsome, compact
male machine and had a sudden intuition that wrestling was

definitely his sport. He laughed again as he opened the car
door and helped her in.

"Naw, I know your dad," he said. "He'd rip my head off.
Let's go get a pizza instead."

The end of the summer found Diane wading in confusion.
A senior in high school, she was determined to take one more
shot at Elite. Many nights she lay awake, her determination
complicated by conflicting adolescent emotions of needing to
be accepted by her peers and insecurity about her own budding
womanhood. Boys at school were noticing that the scrawny,
pig-tailed Diane Ellingson had suddenly, overnight, turned
into a beautiful young woman. No longer shy, she was now
enticingly aloof. There was something appealing in her confident smile and the springy way she carried her body, yet she
was guileless and truly nice to everyone. Everyone knew she
didn't date, but the boys kept hovering closer and closer.

At home alone at night, after school and after the hours
of workout, she would lie in bed and cry from frustration.
School was a plague of uninspiring studies and a bewildering
envy of kids who seemed to have no responsibilities. At times,
she wanted to tear gymnastics from her life, just so she could
breathe. Then sometime during workout, when her muscles
were burning and the rhythm suddenly kicked into place,
another sphere of self-awareness would come into her consciousness. Her mind and heart, her bones and muscles and
nerves, would fuse into a feeling of total invulnerability. Diane
was sure that she could go on forever with this absolute handle
on grace. Gymnastics could never be thrown out of her life,
because it was her life.

So it was a surprise, especially to herself, when Diane

accepted an invitation to the homecoming dance at her school on Friday night.

"How am I going to tell Michelle that I have to leave workout early to go on a date?" Diane had seen the scorn with which Michelle treated other girls who let dating interfere with gymnastics. Would Michelle appreciate Diane's need to have at least some semblance of normal teenage life? There were clearly two things Diane could do: call off the date, or go and not tell Michelle. She thought about the boy. Dave, brown eyes, curly brown hair. She decided to fib to Michelle. Diane suffered so much nervousness over the decision that she barely tasted the pleasure of anticipating the dance. Finally, on Friday afternoon she went to the gym, still wondering what to say to Michelle.

Michelle had taken the day off.

"She's not here?" demanded Diane. "All that worrying, and Michelle isn't even here? Boy!"

The evening was just like in the movies. It was her first real dance, her first time to dress in a party dress and walk under the enchantment of crepe-paper decorations and flickering bee stings of light cast by a mirrored ball hanging from the ceiling. It was her first time to dance with a boy. Dave put his hand on the small of her back and pulled her close. She had never been that close to a boy! He smelled good. She pressed her face against the lapel of his jacket. He whispered, "You really look pretty tonight," his warm voice sending chills down her backbone.

Oh, the heights of romance! Her heart was pounding. The rest of the evening was simply fog—soft, lovely fog.

She fell asleep in his car going home and barely remembered that at the door he didn't kiss her, though she knew he wanted to. She knew only when she woke the next morning that she had a big decision to make.

Dating was too intoxicating. Too enticing. By the time she got to the Academy later that afternoon, she had her mind made up. Boys were definitely poison to gymnastics. No doubt about it. That darling Dave could take her away from it quick as a flash if she let him, and she wasn't going to let him.

So she froze him out. At school she was nice, aloof, friendly, infuriating. If he tried to bring up the subject of another date, she steered the conversation in another direction. He finally got discouraged and stopped asking. Diane felt guilty for hurting someone else to protect herself, but gymnastics was her first love and Diane was loyal. There was no balance.

Still, having chosen her course didn't guarantee a smooth trip. Now that meet season was approaching, the training was harder. She became an assistant coach with the younger kids, which added more pressure to her training schedule, yet she felt grateful for the chance to pay back the coaches at the academy for all they had given her. She came to the gym at one in the afternoon, worked out until four, did endurance training for an hour, taught the young children, and worked out again until 8:30 P.M. On Saturdays she worked out from nine to noon and from two until five.

There were days she balked at the sound of her coaches' voices giving constant, incomprehensible corrections when nothing she tried seemed to do any good. Yet, something held her there like a chain. She hated being in the gym, but when she wasn't in the gym, she hated not being there.

One day, Paul was working with her on the beam. She

couldn't execute the new Elite compulsory dismount, and her frustration telegraphed itself to Paul.

"Do it, Diane. Just do it!"

Time after time she crashed to the floor. Paul told her how to fix it. "You have to twist right off your foot," but she didn't understand him.

"If you don't put out some effort, I won't waste my time," he said. He walked over to Michelle and sat next to her on the stage.

At first, Michelle was patient.

"Try it again, Diane. After you leave the beam, before you hit the top, do a half-twist and then come down."

Diane took a deep breath, pushed off, and ended with an aerial roundoff instead.

"Diane, you've got to wait. Push off your foot, wait, and then turn."

Wait where? In the middle of the air? Diane tried it again and ended up in a roundoff again.

"No, Diane. You've got to twist later!"

Michelle's voice was heating up now, and Diane's mind was freezing. She hated receiving her corrections shouted from across the gym. She tried to initiate the move differently and ended up with a front somersault. She landed on her seat on the floor.

Michelle yelled. "Get back up. Do it again!"

Diane did it again. And again and again and again.

Finally, Michelle came down from the stage, and the whole gym came to a hushed standstill.

"What's the problem, Diane?" she asked the exhausted, stressed girl who stood trembling on the four-inch beam.

"I don't know. I'm trying."

"You've got to concentrate! What's going on in your head? What are you thinking about?"

"I don't know."

How could she think with Michelle standing there? Diane couldn't hear anything but the din of her own frustrations yelling, Why are you so stupid? Why can't you figure this out? Now Michelle is mad at you!

"What did I just say, Diane?" Michelle shouted, bringing Diane back to reality.

"Uhh," Diane said.

"Wanting it just isn't enough. You have to do it! Try it again."

Diane tried again. She landed hard, and through her tears looked over at Paul, begging with her eyes for help. Paul was still sitting on the stage with his arms folded and a lift in his eyebrows that said, "Amen to everything Michelle is saying!"

Nobody in the world wanted to do it right more than Diane did. She closed her eyes, she concentrated, she did it over and over in her mind, and finally, she took off. She sprang from her foot and found herself in the air, unable to make the twist. Michelle reached out to spot her and bodily muscled her into a twist. Diane felt Michelle's rings dig into the flesh of her hip. She landed in a heap.

"Get back up. Do it again."

Diane climbed back up, but courage left her. She stood on the beam and screamed, "I can't get it. Everybody in the gym can get it but me. I'm so mad at myself!"

Michelle screamed right back. "It's my job to coach you. Don't you get mad at yourself. I'll get mad at you. You just listen to me. You do what I tell you! Now, do it again!"

Diane leaped forward without thought, without caring.

She knew she couldn't do it, and she didn't. Again she crumpled to the floor. When she stood, Michelle grabbed her by the shoulders and pushed her toward the door. Diane tripped on a mat and fell against the beam.

"Get out! Get out of this gym," Michelle screamed, and Diane fled.

A few minutes later, Michelle found Diane lying on the stairs crying with wracking, trembling sobs.

Michelle sat down, eased Diane's head onto her lap, and put her arm around her quaking, tiny body.

"D, I know you're frustrated. I know you're discouraged. I was too hard on you, but I know you can do it. We've got to figure this out. We can't give up."

Diane couldn't stop crying. It felt so good to to hear Michelle's voice being soothing and kind. Finally, she was able to say, "Okay. I'm sorry." Michelle's hand felt so gentle on her head.

"Why don't you sit here until you're ready to come back into the gym. Okay?" Michelle stood looking down at Diane.

"Go to the bathroom. Blow your nose."

"Okay."

Diane stumbled into the bathroom. She tried splashing her face with cold water, but forlornly buried her face into the pool of her palms and cried again. All the while she talked to herself, "It's okay, D. Take a deep breath. Calm down," only to lapse into desperation again. Finally, anger began seeping in under the anguish. Diane looked up into the mirror and was appalled by the sight of herself.

"Now I have to go in looking like the biggest idiot."

She doused her face in cold water again, opening her eyes in the water in hopes that the redness would wash away. Even that pain felt better than the bitterness before. Finally, she went back to the gym.

Every eye turned in her direction. She could see the pity and could feel the sympathy from all the other kids. Michelle was standing by the beam. Diane dropped her head and wouldn't look at her.

Michelle put her hands on Diane's shoulders, and said, "Are you calmed down now?"

Diane nodded, still looking at the floor. Michelle put her hand under Diane's chin, lifted her face, and said, "Are you okay? Are you ready to try again now?"

"Yes."

Diane mounted the beam. She was rested now. She decided to try something a little different. This time she pushed off straight forward instead of breaking to the side.

"That's a little better. Try it again this time and push a little harder."

Diane did it again. She did it over and over. Finally, time and space and the presence of the other gymnasts dissolved from her consciousness. The whirring of indistinguishable gym sounds engulfed her. In her mind, she saw Shannon and Jackie and the others doing this same trick. They moved before her in slow motion, gliding along to the end of the beam, taking off from their left foot and twisting to the right.

Diane suddenly snapped back to reality. She had been twisting left off her left foot! Now she knew what was wrong. Paul had told her to twist right off her foot. She had thought he meant right, as in immediately, not right, as in the opposite of left. Well, it didn't matter now. She went to the end of the beam, pushed off, did the twist right, and stuck it!

"Good girl," Michelle said, and she walked away.

What a glorious thing! Diane's soul soared. The tears and frustration were forgotten in the balm of Michelle's approbation. "Good girl," Michelle had said, and Diane was satisfied.

Chapter 6

High school graduation was looming only a few months away. Diane had been offered a full scholarship to the University of Utah by Greg Marsden, the gymnastics coach, but she didn't know whether to take it or not. Truth was, the only goal she had ever had besides gymnastics was to get married, but marriage was not an immediate option, obviously. She was only seventeen. She didn't even have a boyfriend. Her driving goal for the past year had been to make Elite. It had been more of an obsession, actually, than a goal. It was something she felt destined toward, easy to see in her mind, simple to shape her existence around.

Life in the gym was churning up again. One could always tell when meet season was impending because Paul and Michelle became more intense. Intensity was a trait manifested in most coaches, and it was especially apparent to Diane at the Utah Winter Gymnastics Clinic directed by Greg Marsden at the University of Utah. Top coaches from all over the country came to teach different skills, and in two days, Diane saw coaches do things that made her toes curl. They yelled, they lectured, they threw tantrums, they bullied. More than once, she saw a coach hit a recalcitrant gymnast.

"Boy!" Diane whispered to Shannon as the two girls looked on at a coach screaming so hard at one of the boys that the cords were popping out on his neck.

"It never gets like this at the Academy. At least Michelle and Paul don't smack us around!" agreed Shannon.

"Why do we do this sport?" Diane asked.

"Because we love it," said Shannon.

Michelle and Paul were members of the same tough clan of grizzly coaches, no doubt about it, but there wasn't a member of the Academy who hadn't caught them preening with pride over their students' performances or surreptitiously wiping away a tear of sympathy over a luckless fall. Being a top-notch gymnast was seventy-five percent sweat and tears and twenty-five percent fun, but the fun was like gold, precious metal that far outweighed the slag.

Diane opted out of the preliminary Elite season, saving her legs for the last Elite regionals qualifying meet. Two months later, she and Michelle were on the plane to Phoenix. But in spite of a constant prayer that filled every waking moment, Diane failed to qualify. In fact, she was three points off, a truly dismal showing. She was devastated. This had been her last try at Elite. Michelle handed her some sheets of hotel stationery and a pen.

"Write me a report. Tell me how you're feeling."

Diane lay there most of the night, unable to write or think. Making Elite had been the most important thing in her life.

She couldn't possibly imagine going on. Her vision of herself was completely blotted out by the smear of failure.

"Maybe it isn't a big deal to anyone else," Diane prayed, "but gymnastics is my whole life, and now it's ruined. Where do I go from here?"

One after another, her meditations drifted upward, only to hit the ceiling and fall back down like leaden rain. Finally, though, the intense personal introspection gave way to a sudden burning. She sat up, flipped on the light, and began to write.

"How I feel about losing Elite." She brushed away annoying tears. "Michelle, I am really sad about not making Elite. I guess I feel worse than that. It was my dream. I wanted to make you and Paul and Charlie proud and wanted you to think that all your time and money was worth it. I guess I let you down. My dad says that Ellingsons stick to what they start, and I'm no quitter. I've decided that this year I will take the National Class I championship. I'm going to give 100%. I want so much for my training to be worth what you and Paul have given me. I almost feel that I belong to you because I owe you so much. I really love you, and I sort of wish I could stay a little kid my whole life. Love, Diane."

Diane slipped the letter under Michelle's door.

Paul initiated a new training schedule to prepare the girls for Class I regionals. First they worked seven beam routines in a row with thirty seconds between each routine, then three uneven parallel bar sets, and two sets of two back-to-back floor routines. They did optionals one day, compulsories the next. After five minutes' rest, they worked on vaulting horse for about an hour and then worked on parts of routines that needed fine-tuning.

Then came circuit. Ten chin-ups with regular grip, ten
with reverse grip, ten leg lifts with straight legs, ten with bent
knees. Next were twenty handstand pushups against the wall.
After that, while hanging face first over the edge of the trampoline, their feet wound through the springs, they did chest
raises to the count of ten. Then they reversed position, holding
onto the springs with their hands, and did leg raises. Then
twenty-five snap-v situps from the floor. Circuit ended with
fifty kips on the high bar.

Diane found that the new workout schedule reduced most
of the pain in her shins and ankles.

"It's kind of late to be figuring this out now," she said to
herself.

Class I regionals were held in Westminster, California.
Diane went into it confident, fairly free of pain, and determined to win. At the end of the two days of competition, she
stood on the top of the victory stand, the regional Class I all-
around champion!

Her teammates, competitors, and spectators in the gym
thundered, "Yeah, Diane! All right, Diane!" Her head was
swimming with joy. This was just a taste of the miracle she
had prayed for. From Utah, Nevada, Arizona, California, and
Hawaii, she was the all-around champion. It was beyond thrilling—it was electrifying. But instead of feeling gratified, she
felt even more driven. More. She wanted nationals now more
than ever. That night she lay in her motel bed, smiling. Even
in the dark she could see the shadow of the huge regionals
trophy on the dresser.

"It's mine, and I get to take it home," she crooned to
herself. "The one from nationals will even be bigger."

Diane was in top form. For the next three weeks she trained one hundred percent. It was three weeks of the highest, ego-elevating rapture she had ever experienced. She was dredging up talent from the deepest recesses of her sinews. Even her shins and ankles seemed to submit.

"Guess what?" Diane grunted to Shannon as she came through a glide kip halfway through killers at the end of workout one day.

"What?"

"Jim Carlson called me!"

"You're kiddin'. Mr. Popular himself? What did he want?"

"What do you mean, 'What did he want?' ME, of course."

"Uh huh. What else?"

Diane laughed. By now she was so out of breath she could barely talk. "Well . . . he wanted . . . my . . . science notes."

"Yours? Your science notes? That's a laugh."

"Gol, thanks."

"You're welcome."

"He also . . . asked me . . . to . . . go . . . water skiing . . . this . . . weekend."

Diane dropped from the bars and stood doubled over with her hands on her knees for support. The muscles in her forearms and shoulders had knotted up like rocks. She hobbled to the cooler for a drink.

"So, what did you say?"

"Diane! Get over here!" yelled Michelle from across the room. Diane suddenly couldn't swallow.

"What did you say?" repeated Shannon to jog Diane out of her confusion. Shannon never freaked at Michelle's sharp commands, and she wasn't about to let Diane go running away until Diane had answered her question.

"I told him no. It was hard. He's so cute."

"You shouldn't have done that. He'll never ask you again."

"Diane!"

"I know. I really wanted to go with him, but I have to win nationals."

"Well, there oughtta be a way to do both," Shannon started to say, but Diane was already trotting across the floor to Michelle.

Diane forced her shoulders up and back. What trouble was she in now? That command, "Get over here," always meant trouble. Diane was sure she hadn't done anything wrong, so instead of cowering, she looked Michelle in the eyes and smiled until her cheeks stretched across her face.

"Your win at regionals qualified you for the Junior Olympic National Championships in Portland three weeks after nationals," Michelle said.

"That sounds pretty interesting," said Diane. She was more interested, however, in figuring out why she was always so scared when Michelle yelled, "Get over here." She walked away quite excited, not because she'd qualified for Junior Olympics, but because she'd realized that she didn't always have to be afraid when Michelle yelled her name.

Senior nationals was held at Arizona State University. The first day was compulsories. The victory stand was in a corner of the arena. Next to it was a table laden with gold and silver trophies. There was only one Diane was interested in. The biggest.

The warmup period was not long enough. Diane performed

first on the floor and felt lousy. Her score was low enough to match her mood.

"Don't worry about it," Paul told her. "They're scoring low on floor today."

Sure enough, all of the scores were low, and she was in good standing.

She stuck both of her vaults and got a good score, but Paul marched indignantly to the judges table to protest it. He gave reasons why he thought Diane should have received more, but they turned him down.

"That's how it goes," he shrugged. "I tried."

"Thanks," said Diane.

She did her usual good job on bars, but it was on beam that she was really dazzling. Beam was in many ways the most difficult event. Balance had to be perfect. Confidence was everything. Diane scored a 9.5, her highest ever in that event.

After the competition while the coaches were at a meeting, Diane and some of the other girls went back to the hotel restaurant for dinner. Paul walked in, obviously excited about something. He dropped a copy of the meet results in front of her.

"Diane," he said, "your all-around score is in first place."

Half a dozen screaming girls erupted from the table, intertwining around Diane.

"I'm so excited!" Diane yelled. She wished she could call her parents, who had driven to Phoenix the night before and were staying in another motel, but Paul and Michelle absolutely forbade the girls contact with their families during competition.

The next day was May 27. Diane was confident, happy, and enormously proud to walk out onto the floor ranked in first place so far in the meet. National television cameras were on the floor, including those from NBC "Sports World."

"Ladies and gentlemen," boomed the voice of the meet announcer. "We'd like to extend a special congratulations to Diane Ellingson. Today is her eighteenth birthday!"

The audience applause echoed in the curved beams of the stadium ceiling. The telescoping lenses of television cameras followed her every reaction. Diane kept thinking that she ought to be embarrassed, but truthfully, she loved it.

"What do you want for your birthday?" the commentator asked Diane, moving in for a live interview.

"That first-place trophy over there!"

Diane started on the vaulting horse. Her move wasn't a difficult one — she stuck both landings — and smiled into the cameras that were still dogging her.

Next was the beam.

Diane's mount on the beam was to run, jump off the spring board, do a half-twist, and land in a handstand on the beam with her legs in a full split. Then she'd turn a complete circle and step down on the end of the beam to continue the routine.

She performed the mount, the pirouette, stepped down on the end of the beam, and hit a perfect pose.

Then something caught her eye. Not twenty feet from her on the sideline was the cutest guy she had ever seen, and he was looking right at her. He smiled. Diane knew from his stance that he was a gymnast, and she also knew that if he was going to talk to her at the end of the meet she would have to impress him.

Balancing on the beam in front of national television cameras, nationally ranked judges in official uniform, her parents, and everybody in the crowd, she thought only about impressing one guy. She checked to see if he was still watching, and he was. She moved into the next part of her routine, the hardest part, and executed it perfectly.

Was he still looking? Yes. Suddenly, bits of a conversation she had had with her dad the night before the meet flashed into her mind.

"I'll be eighteen in two days."

"Never mind that, young lady," her dad had said. "That doesn't mean you know anything about men."

It was true. She had not had the experience of high school locker room gossip. She had had only two dates and had never yet been kissed by a boy. She had never seen even one steamy episode of an afternoon soap opera or gone to a movie racier than PG.

"Marie, do you know about sex and all of that stuff?" she asked her sister later.

Marie, who was fifteen, snorted in disgust and said, "Diane, even Louise knows more about it than you do."

Now, because of that split second loss of concentration on her easiest trick, a full turn on one foot, Diane slipped and fell off the beam.

Panicked, she jumped back up, but before she could take another step, she fell off the other side.

She looked over. The guy was gone.

She performed the rest of her routine without a hitch, turned to face the cameras with thousands of people watching, and smiled her best smile.

She felt like an idiot. She muttered to herself in bitter jest, "I hope the judges didn't notice that I fell off twice."

They noticed. Her score reflected a point lost for two falls.

"It's okay, it's okay," Paul said as he handed her a towel. "You still have bars. You're nationally known for bars. You came into this thing more than a point ahead of everybody else. You can still do it."

Diane was grateful that Michelle wasn't there. She would have seen her look at that boy. Sure as anything, she would have seen it. Still able to muster some dignity, knowing that she was one of the few gymnasts in the country who could perform her particular mount, a front somersault over the low bar to catch the high bar, she chalked up her hands and tested the tension of the guy wires. Then she took a deep breath, ran, jumped off the spring board, turned the somersault over the low bar, and reached for the high bar.

She missed it by half an inch.

Although a thirty-second remount time is allowed in this case, in which most gymnasts take the opportunity to catch their breath, chalk up again, and pull themselves together, Diane ricocheted off the floor and up onto the bars the instant she realized what she had done. From then on, she performed a perfect, spectacular, gorgeous routine.

This time Paul didn't say anything when he handed her the towel. She looked at his pained face and said, "Do you think they noticed? Only a trained eye could have seen me hit that floor before I was back up there."

"Nope," he grinned. "I didn't see anything." The judges noticed, however, and her score showed it.

Diane went through her floor routine in a daze. She came off to appreciative applause and said to Paul, "Well, at least I didn't fall off the floor."

At the end of the second day of competition, she was in sixth place.

Actually, things weren't so bad. Sixth would still earn her a place on the victory stand. The second-day meet results showed that she was only two-tenths of a point behind the girl in first place. She could make that up. The pressure would be off. First of all, it wouldn't be her birthday anymore, and the television cameras would be tagging along somebody else's tail now. She could just concentrate on sneaking that title right out from under everyone's noses.

But the next day Diane's plan to pull off a surprise win disintegrated. It was the beam again! Even without the cute guy to distract her, she missed the same move. Taking first place in the all-around was impossible now, and Diane scrambled to find some hope. She was desperate not to leave this meet a failure. If she could just stay on bars, she might be able to squeeze out a trophy on that one event.

She jumped off the spring board, turned the somersault over the low bar, reached for the high bar, and caught it exactly right!

Perfect timing! The mount was the hardest part of the routine and she knew she was home free.

The next major move was a handstand on the high bar with a half-turn. She came out of the handstand to whip the low bar, popped into a backup-rise, free-hip handstand, then whipped the bar again and snapped into a front somie. She performed the somie, flew clear above the high bar, turned over, and caught it exactly right. She heard the audience clapping. There was nothing like the approval of an audience to jazz up a performance.

"Finally, something is working," she thought to herself.

Diane's dismount was a hecht off the high bar over the low bar. She had to wrap around the high bar and then pop off at about a forty-five degree angle, fly over the high bar, over the low bar, and land about a foot in front of the low bar.

She popped off the high bar, but instead of going off at a forty-five degree angle, she shot straight up. Coming down, she hit her feet on the high bar, banged her shins on the low bar, and landed, splat! in a grand belly-flop, face down, on the mat.

The stadium was silent as a tomb.

Diane peeled herself off the mat while stars flew around in her head. She didn't know if her nose was poking into or out of her face.

At the end of a routine, gymnasts are required to present themselves to the judges. Diane turned and gave them a crooked smile.

They were laughing! They were trying hard not to, but they couldn't believe what they had just seen.

Diane turned to the stunned audience, jacked up the grin on her face, and waved. Sporadic, weak clapping broke loose, which crescendoed into a roar. Diane looked for her parents. There they were, giving her a standing ovation. Diane was sure their hearts must have been breaking.

With her smile still pasted on, she walked past the other gymnasts on the floor, down the corridor to the locker room, and collapsed into a corner, glad that Paul couldn't follow her there.

She had just blown the biggest chance of her life. She had worked, she had trained, she had suffered. She had given so much for so long and now, just when it should have all paid off, everything fell apart.

"Why am I always crying my eyes out in bathrooms?" she asked herself. Somehow or other she pulled together whatever crumbs of self-respect she had left and dragged herself out just in time to do her floor routine. Her performance was respectable enough to earn her eighth place in that event.

For the rest of the day she smiled, offering congratulations to others, playing down her own feelings. Coaches and other gymnasts complimented her on her good sportsmanship. She was offered scholarships to three universities that day. During finals on bars that evening she sat on the bleachers and watched other girls get better scores than she did with routines half as good as hers. She was furious with herself. After working so hard and sticking so many in a row week after week, it just wasn't fair.

Later, the cute boy, the one who had ruined her life, came up to her in the hotel lobby and asked her to go for a walk.

His name was Russ, and yes, he was a gymnast on a men's college team. He had a birthday present for Diane, a small plaque with a mirror in the center that said, "You're looking at a winner."

She walked with him to the parking lot where they sat on the hood of his car. They talked about the meet.

"I'm so mad at myself for blowing it so bad," she said.

"Well, you acted like a winner."

"You think so?" she asked, looking at him. She hadn't noticed how close he had moved toward her. Suddenly, his arm went around her shoulders, and he pressed his face into the hair behind the back of her ear.

"You're a winner in my book," he whispered.

She flew off the hood of the car.

"What are you doing?"

He sat with his jaw hanging, his eyes big as plums. "I want to kiss you," he said.

"Well, I don't want to kiss you!"

For a moment she thought about apologizing for hurting his feelings but decided not to. She turned and fled into the hotel.

What did he expect? I hardly know him! Those were the things she said to herself, but what she knew in her heart was that she was both scared and disappointed. She had wanted to kiss that boy. Even that one, who was the cause of all her sorrows. She longed for the awakening of it. Why couldn't there be room for both gymnastics and romance in her life?

The next day, after a miserable, sleepless night, Diane flew home. She had started out the first day of this competition in first place, favored to win the national championship. She went home in twenty-sixth place.

Chapter 7

Four days later, Diane stood in white cap and gown, inconspic-
uous among hundreds of other Olympus High School seniors
whom she barely knew, graduating from a school she had never
been much a part of. Her locker partner sat next to her. She
didn't even know her very well, although they had shared
friendly moments for three years, greeting each other between
classes, sharing small bits of laughter or frustration.

Diane wandered around, feeling lost in a sea of white and
kelly green flowing robes. The ceremonies were held on the
football field. No wonder she felt lost. She had never once
been to this place to enjoy its primary function. Not one
football game in three years. She had never been to a basketball
game or any other such after-school activity.

The next day at workout, Michelle told Diane that Junior
Olympics might be cancelled.

Typical. What had she worked for all these years, these
past weeks, the last few days? Nothing. She had come home

a loser from nationals. The other girls were all through with competitions, gearing down for summer training. She was still working out, keeping her endurance up, and sharpening her routines. For what?

"The girls in the east are boycotting the meet because it's being held in Oregon, and it was held in the West last year," Michelle said.

Those spoiled brats. Diane suddenly resented the possibility of not going to that meet. More than anything else, she wanted to do well there. She had to have something worthwhile to hang her past on. And now, after years of sweat, she was being told that Junior Olympics probably wouldn't be held because a bunch of back East babies was boycotting it. She jumped to the high bar and started pounding out her routine. It was a good one; she had plenty of energy but was out of heart. Anger began driving her through the motions, and suddenly she had so much power that she lost control on a front somersault, bashed both legs on the high bar, and fell between the bars on her back.

She didn't dare cry. Both Paul and Michelle stood over her with their arms folded, looking like bouncers waiting to throw her out of the gym.

"You have to get up and do it again now, Diane," Paul said, "before you can quit doing bars."

Diane was exhausted, but she still did it perfectly. It was an easy trick by now.

Michelle followed her out of the gym, put her arm around her shoulders and said, "Come on, Diane. We have to talk about this."

In Michelle's office Diane let flood a stream of tears. She was burned out. "I'm tired of gymnastics."

Diane winced at her own blasphemy. Tired of gymnastics! How dare she profane Michelle's religion! She waited for Michelle to get angry, but Michelle put both her hands on Diane's knees and looked deep into her eyes. "It's okay, Diane. Everybody gets burned out. Do you need a vacation?"

Diane's mouth opened. "How long a vacation?"

The very thought of it felt like Disneyland in her soul. Vacation? Oh, yes. Forever!

"Oh, I don't know. A week. Two weeks. A month. Diane, it's no disgrace if you want to quit."

Paul stood in the doorway. "You can't quit!" he said. "You'd better think about this until Monday." He turned and left the room.

Michelle's hands still rested on Diane's knees. "All I want is for you to be happy. Whether you're a gymnast or not, I want you to be happy."

"Okay," Diane said. She went home that night and slept like the dead. There would be no disgrace if she quit forever. Michelle would still love her.

But the next morning she woke in a foul mood. She got out her journal and listed all the reasons she should quit gymnastics and all the reasons she should not.

The "I should quit!" list was a long one. She was sick and tired. She couldn't face her routines anymore. She was gagging on her coaches telling her what to do all the time. She was mentally burned out. Her ankles hurt. Her shins hurt. She hated vaulting. She hated beam worse. The bars were boring. There were rips in her hands. Diane wrote with a fever. The list grew. She had never been to a football game. She had never kissed a boy.

When there was nothing hateful left to think of, she sat

looking at the list. She stared at it. Finally, she flipped to a clean sheet and wrote, "Why I should keep training in case they hold Junior Olympics."

She remembered a poem by Walter Wintle hanging on the Academy wall:

> If you think you're beaten, you are.
> If you think you dare not, you don't.
> If you'd like to win but you think you can't,
> It's almost a cinch you won't.
> If you think you'll lose, you're lost.
> For out in the world we find,
> Success begins with a fellow's will.
> It's all in his state of mind.
> Life's battles don't always go
> To the stronger or faster man,
> But sooner or later the one who wins,
> Is the one who thinks he can.

On the clean page Diane wrote, "I am a champion, not a quitter."

The next day, when Paul and Michelle arrived at the Academy, they found Diane sitting on the front steps waiting for them.

"I just want you to know," Diane said, "that I really love you." She picked up her gym stuff and walked ahead of them into the gym.

That day she learned that Junior Olympics was on after all.

"To think I almost quit right at the end," she thought to herself.

On June 10, Diane and Paul arrived in Portland, Oregon. Diane spent most of the night unable to sleep, berating herself for not having any enthusiasm. What was the matter with her? She had given her all in practice every day, had tried to psych herself up every night, but the old desire just wasn't there. Finally, to avoid conversing with her own negative thoughts, she opened her Bible to read. Her eyes stuck to every word, lingered, and trudged on uncomprehending. She persisted. Eventually, the words began slipping past her eyes into her head. Like warm fluid, the words washed across her mind; it seemed they were reading her. Finally, she dropped off to sleep with the sweetest feeling of contentment she had known in months. God loves me. I'll compete in this meet for him. Not for me. For him.

The next day she was relaxed, almost nonchalant about the whole thing. With her mind shut down, her body took over. The past few weeks of training had honed her to razor-sharp precision. At the end of the first day, she was in second all around, close at the heels of the girl in first place.

Paul took her sightseeing the next day. She had French toast for breakfast, cotton candy at the zoo for lunch, and no dinner. They returned to the hotel late, missed their ride to the gym, had to take a taxi, and arrived just as the two-hour warm-up period was beginning. Diane flopped down on a mat to rest her eyes and fell sound asleep. Paul let her lie there. Finally, he woke her.

"Hey, lazy, get up. You've got an hour to warm up."

When the meet began, Diane was tempted to look over in the direction of the victory stand to check out the trophies but forced herself not to.

Her vault score was not the highest but it was close. Her bar routine was as flawless as she had ever done, but halfway through it, she hit her knee on the spring board that had been left under the bars. The accident stopped Diane's momentum. Paul leaped up, moved the board, and Diane glided right back into her routine, finishing it with a flourish, and presented herself to the judges with a big smile.

They must have been impressed with the overall routine. In spite of losing half a point for the mishap, she scored a 9.4.

Most of the girls were feeling the pressure by now, and many of them washed out on beam. But Diane felt superbly calm. Her routine was solid with hardly a wiggle through any of it.

She posed on the floor, waiting for the music to start, facing herself in the mirrored wall alongside the mat. In that brief moment, she beamed at herself and whispered, "You're cookin' now, Big Bird."

The music started. She put the maximum extension and amplitude into the moves and nodded in full approval when she ended to the exact last beat of the music.

When it was all over, Diane knew she had done well in this meet. After the last gymnast performed, all the competitors walked out onto the floor to receive a long-stemmed red rose and a small loving cup that said "Junior Olympic National Championship." Then they marched around the floor and sat down on the edge of the mat while the victory stand was set up under an arch of roses.

The junior division winners were announced first and then the senior division winners.

"In vaulting . . . " the announcer's voice boomed as it ran rapidly through the list, naming the sixth, fifth, fourth, third, and " . . . second place, Diane Ellingson!"

Diane took her place to the right of the top step on the

victory stand. She accepted her silver trophy, shook hands with the official, and beamed in the direction of the judges.

No sooner had she and the other winners filed off the victory stand than the announcer began reading off the winners of the uneven parallel bar competition. Sixth, fifth, fourth, third, second — Diane had known all along that her name would be announced — first! She flew to the victory stand this time and accepted the larger, gold trophy.

"And now, the balance beam winners," said the announcer. "In sixth place. . ." His voice ran on, "fifth, . . . fourth, . . . third . . . ." Diane's leg muscles tightened to rise. "Second." Diane watched another girl run up to stand on the second step. The announcer spoke " . . . and, first, Diane Ellingson!"

Again she stood on the top of the victory stand. She received her third trophy, and now her face was beginning to hurt from smiling. The judges returned her salute, she sat down, glancing around at Paul with an expression that said, "Is this a miracle, or what?"

Paul sidled up behind her and said, "I never thought I'd see the day that you'd win a national title on beam."

"Me either," Diane said.

The announcer was already naming the winners of the floor exercise. "Sixth, . . . fifth, . . . fourth, . . . third . . . "

Diane caught her breath.

" . . . second, Diane Ellingson!"

For the fourth time, Diane marched up to the victory stand. She stood, accepted her trophy, and this time when she looked at the judges, she laughed with delight. She could not keep herself from it.

Back sitting on the floor, Diane thought to herself, "Okay,

I'm either first or second in the all-around." She could hardly contain her excitement.

"In the all-around competition . . . "

The names of the sixth-, fifth-, fourth-, and third-place winners escaped her. She strained to hear her name. No, second place went to another girl. That could only mean . . . ! Diane suddenly pictured the Miss America Pageants. "Oh, gag," thought Diane. "I hate Miss America!"

"First place in the all-around goes to Miss Diane Ellingson!"

First place! Miss America!

Diane jumped to the top of the victory stand. She received roses, a plaque, and a huge loving cup. The announcer's voice proclaimed, "Diane Ellingson, our new Junior Olympic national champion. Congratulations, Diane."

She began to tremble inside. All she could think of was that she had nearly quit. She had had every good reason in the world, but she hadn't quit, and now here she was, at the top of the victory stand. Elation poured through her, and she basked in her place on top of the world. Paul stood on the sidelines, grinning with pride.

The girls lined up, saluted the judges and spectators, and marched off the floor. Diane went straight to Paul and slugged him in the shoulder.

"Did you know I was going to win?"

"Yes. I was adding up the scores."

"Why didn't you tell me?"

"The last time I told you you were going to win, you fell apart. I wasn't about to do that again."

Crowds of people suddenly converged, congratulating Diane. One of the judges gave her the corsage from her lapel.

Another judge whispered in her ear, "I judged your first Elite qualifying meet. You've still got that beautiful smile and amazing attitude. Congratulations."

The rest of the evening passed all too quickly just that way. Diane was overwhelmed with the attention, mouths talked at her from all directions, lips brushed her cheeks, arms hugged her. She was interviewed by the local newspapers, radio, and television stations and by writers from *International Gymnastics* magazine and *Gymnastics World*. She hardly tasted a bite of dinner because of the number of people who interrupted to offer congratulations. Her head was whirling by the time she finally found herself alone in her room. Sitting on the dresser, like a line of sentinels, were her six trophies, the plaque, and the spray of red roses. She took a photograph and then dropped to her knees to say thanks.

Chapter 8

When Diane lost at nationals, it seemed that life, like a stream of fresh water, had been sucked down into the stagnant recesses of a dead pool. She might have drowned had the undercurrents of raw talent and determination not been stirred.

Breaking away to test the flow once more at Junior Olympics had caught her up and sent her swirling headlong to the crest of gymnastics success. That moment of glory was hers. She was Junior Olympic National Champion! Happiness stood suspended, like a wave that seems to pause in full curl before the inevitable ebb draws it back to fill the tide.

Diane knew that if she could keep up the momentum, if she stayed with the Academy instead of going to college, she would make Elite. She knew it, and that was enough. The view from the crest had given her a clear perspective. Making Elite was only that—another moment of glory, a wave crashing in on itself.

Diane decided instead to channel gymnastics to carry her

into the future. She stayed with the Academy the rest of that summer, but in August she registered for classes at the University of Utah. To Michelle and other Elite gymnasts, it was a step down for her. To Diane, it was a step away; away from childhood, away from Michelle's apron strings. Diane loved Michelle, but now she found herself balking at her control and disagreeing with the way she and Paul did certain things.

One day Diane and Shannon decided to go for frozen yogurt at lunchtime. They saw Michelle eating her lunch alone in her car, but when they asked her to go with them, she refused.

They walked on across the street, but Diane kept looking back. She had the urge to run back and sit with Michelle. She could press Michelle to find out what was bothering her and at least let her know that she cared, but she followed Shannon across the street like a coward.

And yet, when Michelle and Paul were in Las Vegas at the National Coaches Congress on Diane's last day at the Academy, it seemed almost like a betrayal. How could they just go on with business as usual when she was leaving? How could she leave without telling them everything in her heart?

Diane tearfully said good-bye to all of her old friends, feeling as she walked out the door that her heart was being torn from her. Her knees went weak, and she crumpled onto the steps. This place, these people, had meant so much to her. They would all go on as usual in their safe, controlled harbor, while Diane was heading out toward open sea.

She picked up her things and stood in the heavy waves of late afternoon sun. Everything cast long, flat shadows. Things looked strange outside the gym. Too big.

Within days after she left the Academy, Greg Marsden was on the phone, asking if she'd like to come in and work out with the University of Utah team. Could the transition really be that easy? Yesterday she was a student at the Utah Academy of Gymnastics, and today, a Lady Ute? No fanfare, no ceremony?

Diane had known Greg Marsden for several years. He was gaining a reputation in Utah gymnastics and across the country. He inspired a kinetic kind of winning drive in his athletes.

Greg had offered to pick her up. When she opened the door to him, he said, "I have a surprise for you."

Shannon leaped out from around the side of the house where she had been hiding. The two girls erupted into screams and hugs of delight.

"What are you doing?"

"I quit the Academy, too," Shannon laughed. "No way was I gonna hang around there all by myself."

Greg drove along Foothill Boulevard and talked about some of the things they should expect. Diane and Shannon politely ignored him, unable to absorb more than the excitement of being together after all.

"But you're still in high school, Shannon. How did you work it?" Diane asked.

"Well, I'm not actually gonna be on the team. Just work out and do my own thing at the Elite meets. Greg said it'd be okay."

"What did Michelle say?"

"You don't want to hear."

"Yes I do."

"No you don't."

Although built above ground, the cement and brick corridors of the Health, Physical Education, and Recreation building, called the HPER by the students, seemed like an enormous bomb shelter. Long, windowless halls and tiled floors stretched away to the vanishing point. On one side was a basketball gym; on the other, various doors opened up into weight rooms or classrooms, stairways or racquetball courts. A hallway jutted to the right; a smaller passageway housing coaching offices and supply closets opened to the left. Numerous sweaty, well-muscled boys wearing frayed, cut-off gray sweat clothes and similarly toned girls with bouncing ponytails jogged by.

"Were you in gymnastics up here, Greg?" Diane asked.

"Hah! No. I never did gymnastics. I was a diver."

Shannon and Diane looked at each other. Shannon silently mouthed the words, "Never did gymnastics?"

Greg went on, "Besides, they don't have men's gymnastics here. Just women's."

Greg opened the double doors to the workout gym. Diane suddenly remembered that first magical glimpse of the Academy gym four years ago, and a great longing filled her. This University of Utah gym was perfect—fitted out with the best equipment—but would it ever be dear to her? She grimaced with real sadness, thinking how she had not actually said goodbye to Michelle and Paul, nor had she had a chance to thank them as they deserved. A feeling of traitorous guilt chilled her.

When Greg introduced her and Shannon to the other gymnasts, Diane sensed a touch of animosity crackle the air. She couldn't blame them, knowing that they were wondering how these new gymnasts would affect the balance of their program. Gymnastics was developing so rapidly as a sport that it was almost taken for granted that each year the new gymnasts would be better than the old ones. Greg's gymnasts all knew who Shannon and Diane were: Shannon, the first and best

Elite gymnast in Utah, and now Diane, United States Junior Olympic champion, the one local sportscasters were already calling "Greg Marsden's best girl."

Greg smiled. He sent Shannon off to warm up and ushered Diane into the training room cage, a narrow fenced-in area off to the side with a bench, lockers and equipment, and a small refrigerator-freezer for ice packs. The other end of the cage was outfitted with medical supplies, tape, braces, and heat packs for use by the trainers.

"Diane, this is Tyler, our team trainer. You'll get to know each other very well. He has a therapy plan that's going to save your gymnastics career."

Starting that moment, Diane was put on a strict, daily training-room schedule that she adhered to faithfully for the next four years. An hour and a half before the other gymnasts arrived for workout, Diane was in the whirlpool working her ankles up and down, around and around, warming them up in the wet heat. When she got out of the pool, she stood on a slant board for ten to fifteen minutes to stretch the Achilles tendons until they were loose. Tyler then taped her ankles and shins in a way he had developed especially for her.

"This will reinforce the tendons . . . protect them so they can build up," he said as he grunted over his work, carefully pulling and stretching the tape to just the right tautness, smoothing it down evenly across, around, and over Diane's legs.

"What spindles. It's a wonder you ever survived the pain. I can feel the scar tissue with my fingers."

After her ankles were taped, Diane would lie on her stomach with a moist-heat hydroculator pad warming her lower back for about fifteen minutes, after which she carefully stretched, easing into back bends and arches until she was as warm and limber as a cat. Then, dressed in knee socks, sweat pants, and shirt, she sat in the sauna in the women's locker room until her body was hot from top to toe.

Back in the locker room, still dressed in sweats, she stretched again to warm up every muscle. She got into the gym about half an hour before the others arrived and ran around the floor mat to get her legs and ankles going, finally finishing up with several minutes of dance on the beam.

Without this daily ritual, she couldn't make it through an entire workout session. When someone asked why she put up with the hassle, she said, "You do whatever it takes." Sometimes, though, when the other girls came bouncing in ten minutes before workout, threw on some gym clothes, and hit the training without flinching a bit, she wondered if it was worth it.

Just one week after she started training with the university, Shannon was forced to quit, policy forbidding a nonstudent to work out with the team. Instead of going back to the Academy, she opted to move away to live with another Elite gymnast in California and train with a top coach there. Diane felt bad for her, but it wasn't uncommon in gymnastics for the best Elite gymnasts to do just that.

Diane's scholarship included room and board in the dorms, but at first she preferred to live at home. In the mornings her father dropped off her sisters at high school and Diane at the university on his way to work. In the evening, he came by the gym to pick Diane up. It became a routine that she relished. Many times she came out to the car to find a shiny apple waiting on the seat for her. "Oh, Dad, thanks," Diane would say as she wolfed down the apple. "You're welcome," he'd say, always shy of fuss.

University life seemed too good to be true. Diane had classes in the morning until ten, and then for the first time in her life, she had nothing to do. She watched television in the Union Building or stretched out on the lawns in the hot September sun with her pant legs rolled up. At one it was time to go to the gym. She warmed up for her usual hour and a half and then worked out until six. She lazed around at home, too. It was great.

Then one day, Greg called her into his office.

"Diane, I got a copy of your midterm grades."

"You did?"

"There's something you should know: I get your grades before you do. Diane, it's a privilege to have a scholarship to this university, and you have to get above a 2.0 grade point average to keep it. How bad do you want to be on this team? You get good grades or you're out of here, and I have nothing to say about it. You're not a kid anymore. You have to be responsible for your own life."

The pressure hit suddenly, like a flash flood. Why hadn't she seen the clouds coming up over the horizon? It was already midterm, and Diane was suddenly drowning in unfinished work, barely floating on D grades. Getting A's and B's in high school had not given her good study habits for college. "I should have been at the library all that time I've been messing around," she berated herself.

One night after days of struggle to catch up her grades, Diane closed the bedroom door behind her and looked around. The walls were covered with gymnastics posters and pages of old gymnastics magazines. Another wall held her trophy case jammed with trophies and ribbons. A corner of the room was heaped with stuffed Big Birds. Diane turned her radio full blast to the loudest rock station she could find and then screamed as loud as she could. She put her head into her pillow and screamed some more. She hated gymnastics, hated school, hated looking at all those posters and junk. They all stood for something that she used to be and loved, and now she hated it. It was all stale.

Finally, she went to the garage and returned with some boxes into which she jammed everything. The empty walls closed in on her. She thought of Michelle and mourned for her in great sobs.

"I wish things could be like they were. That first year at the Academy was so thrilling and I was so in love with gymnastics. I loved life then, and I hate it now."

She picked up her sociology book. She hated that class! She threw the book across the room.

Later she focused her animosity at Greg, keeping her resentment smouldering inside. She went to classes feeling more buried than ever. At the same time, workout was getting more intense in preparation for meet season in January. Greg could be as ornery as Paul and Michelle when under pressure.

One day he yelled at Diane when she was working on bars.

"You're not even trying. You're just messing around up there. Quit falling off."

He ordered her to do two routines in a row, rest five minutes, do them again, and then repeat the sequence over and over until he said it was enough. She puffed and grunted, getting more and more angry. Greg ignored her theatrics. She started to hyperventilate. Greg walked away. Diane threw herself on the floor, gasping for breath. Finally the trainer put a paper bag over her face.

When she was finally breathing normally again, Greg yelled from across the gym, "Get up off the floor, Diane."

Diane felt sick. She resolved not to let her anger show anymore.

A few weeks later, she flew to Cody, Wyoming, to participate in a gymnastics clinic with Greg. She demonstrated every move while he spotted her. Later, Greg asked her to speak to the nearly one hundred kids who were there."They've never seen a gymnast as good as you before."

Diane told them the things she thought were most important: "You have to do a lot of routines, over and over, without getting discouraged," she said. "You have to have a positive attitude. You should be friendly and positive towards other gymnasts. When performing, always look your best, have confidence, and believe in yourself."

Diane hesitated. Did she really believe all of that? Yes, she did. She should have been talking to herself like this lately. She looked at the sidelines and saw Greg standing there, his arms folded, smiling at her.

Diane and Greg talked about her grades on the flight home.

"You'll be on academic probation after this quarter, Diane, but I can help you. Next quarter you can sign up for a couple of my classes and we'll see if you can get your grades up. But you better show up for class and study, because I'm not giving you good grades for nothing."

That night, Diane put the posters back up on her walls and filled the trophy case again, but the Big Bird toys she left tucked away in her closet. She let go of Paul and Michelle as her coaches. Greg was her coach now.

Meet season that year was a dream. Diane was unequivocally the best member of the team, doing well enough on all the events to take the all-around title in almost every Western Athletic Conference meet. She garnered media attention. It was seldom that her picture did not appear in the newspaper or on a television camera in connection with a meet. Her legs felt good, and her focus was on winning.

Greg badgered them all about teamwork, but Diane could not see how her winning could hurt the team. Coming in first all-around in every meet meant more to her than anything. Then a few weeks before regionals, during a coaching class demonstrating for Greg, Diane smacked the top of her foot into the springboard. The pain was stifling, but she swallowed her complaints, knowing that if her injury were bad enough, Greg would scratch her from competition and she would lose her chance at the national individual all-around title. During the next meet, she fell on her neck from the bars and went around for the next few days with a headache. At the same meet, she jammed her ankles into the mat twice during warmups but didn't say anything then, either, and pushed herself to win the all-around. She couldn't even walk by the time she got home. Greg was furious with her for keeping her injuries secret and made her lay off almost entirely for the next ten days of workout.

The last big competition of the year before regionals was Utah vs. Cal-State Fullerton and Southwest Missouri. Fullerton's team was one of the top in the nation. Since the meet was to be held in Utah, Greg called in the media during workout the week before the meet. All three major television stations and three local newspapers came with their cameras, invading every corner of the gym. The University of Utah *Chronicle* did a cover story about Diane. The media came again on the day of the meet, interviewing Kathy Rigby, retired Olympic star, who was doing commentary on the meet for national broadcast coverage. Diane, who was a ham in front of cameras, attracted the most attention. Even though she hadn't worked out for almost two weeks, she was determined to take the all-around.

Warmups went well. Utah started out on the vaulting horse. Diane threw a tsukahara and landed her first vault. It hurt her foot a little bit. She did another tsuke for her second vault. This time the landing hurt like the blazes, but she hid the pain behind a big smile, went over to the side, and put a bag of ice on her foot, covering it with a towel so no one in the audience would see that she was hurt, Greg especially.

The next event was bars. Diane scuttled her usual mount because it hurt too much to run and jump off the springboard. Instead, she did a glide kip catch for the mount and from there went on to a flawless performance, the best she had ever done.

Diane's score on bars came up the best, but her grin disappeared when she stood to walk and she realized that the dismount from the bars had been the last straw. She couldn't walk at all.

Tyler took her back to the training room, iced the swollen foot, and gave her aspirin. Greg scratched her from the rest of the meet.

Diane was sitting in the training room crying, when Greg walked back in.

"Diane," he said, his eyes smouldering, "you're not the

only one being hurt by this. You better cheer up and get out there and support your team."

She dried her eyes, forced a smile, and went out to watch her team fall apart. The loss of their star performer and her scores on beam and floor knocked the wind out of Utah's sails. They ended up in third place.

Paul and Michelle were in the audience. They, who were so down on college gymnastics, had come to see her perform. They came down to the floor, and Michelle put her arm around Diane. "There was nothing wrong with that bar routine. You should have had a 10."

Diane went to bed that night longing for Michelle and Paul and regretting her own bad luck.

In the morning she called Greg to tell him that she couldn't walk. He drove her to the doctor. Her metatarsals were badly sprained, and once again she was out because of injury. Greg seemed almost as depressed about it as she.

"It looks like your whole life is going to be spent fighting back, Diane."

"I guess so."

Later she told him, "There is one bright spot in all of this. Laying off working out for the last three weeks has maybe killed my gymnastics, but it saved my college career. I've studied my eyeballs out, and I'm all caught up."

"That's great," said Greg, "but I don't think your gymnastics career is over. Tell me honestly. Do you think you could land one dismount on bars at regionals?"

"I guess," laughed Diane. "I probably wouldn't be able to walk away from it, though."

"That's okay, I'll carry you. If you want to do bars at regionals, you can go."

"Seriously?"

"Yeah."

Diane went, performed only on bars, and took the gold medal in that event. Her team earned a berth at nationals.

Psyched into believing she could play catch-up again, Diane decided to train for nationals. Tyler told her that riding a bicycle would be good for her ankles and foot. She withdrew her savings from the bank to buy a new ten-speed. The next day she rode it the eight miles from her home to the university. When she entered the gym later, Greg had a grin on his face.

"Just because you got your picture on the cover of a national magazine doesn't mean you can walk into practice any old time you want."

"What are you talking about?"

He showed her his March issue of *Gymnastics World*. There she was doing a split leap on the cover. Diane flushed. Being famous could be a real treat.

It wasn't until they got to nationals in Seattle, though, that Diane learned that gymnasts had to qualify with an all-around score at regionals to compete all-around at nationals. She'd counted heavily on winning the all-around at nationals, and her disappointment showed.

"Who are you here for, Diane?" Greg asked. "Yourself, or the team?"

Diane knew that if she said the wrong thing, he would jerk her right out of the competition.

"I'm here for the team," she said, but it was a lie. She had come to win for herself first, the team second. But what was good for her was good for the team, wasn't it?

Then, as if in answer to the question, during warm-up on beam, she pushed off wrong on her bad foot for the dismount and reinjured it. A decent score from her on all events would have greatly helped the team. As it was, she had to scratch all the events except bars.

The meet consisted of two parts, the preliminary meet for team scores and the finals for individual honors. Even with her injury, Diane's performance on bars assured her team sixth place in the national standings, up from tenth place the year before.

Individual finals were a disaster for her, however. All day people had been telling her she would win bars because she was the best bar worker in the country. She fell off in the middle of her routine and ended up taking ninth place out of ten. She smiled, covering up her intense humiliation and disappointment. She was a good sport in front of the crowd, but when she got back to her room at the hotel she broke down.

Winning that title had meant everything to her. The more she cried, the angrier she got, until she was telling herself once again that she hated gymnastics.

A knock came at the door. It was Greg. By this time, she was so far gone in self-pity that she didn't care if he saw it. "What makes this all worth it?" she asked him.

"I haven't accomplished one thing with you this year, have I?" Greg asked. "You don't have to be number one to make this a worthwhile experience."

Diane knew that Greg was controlling his temper. He put his arm around her shoulders.

"I don't know if you'll believe me or not, but I'm going to tell you anyway. It's not the trophies or awards or honors that you win for yourself that count. Those things are just trinkets. What matters is that you learn what it takes to be a

great athlete and a good team player. Then you can go anywhere in life and be a successful person. If you don't learn
that—you're right: your years as a gymnast are wasted. Totally
meaningless. Gymnastics is an avenue, not a destination."

That night she thought about what he said. She thought
about Nancy Theis and what made her great. Diane made a
promise to herself. The next day she told Greg, "From now
on, it's the team first."

"That's super," he said. "Diane, we need to know what
we can count on. If you're injured, you have to think enough
of the team to let somebody else fill in. Believe me, if everybody
on the team has that attitude, we'll take nationals someday.
We'll be number one. All of us. Wait and see."

Diane nodded and started to walk away.

"By the way, you made All-American."

She turned around. "What's that? Do I get anything?"

"No. You're so greedy. There's no hardware in it. It's a
title. It means you were among the top ten in the nation all
year, that's all."

Diane grinned. "Oh, is that all?"

Chapter 9

The instant she hit the water, Diane felt the sudden impulse to panic. Instead, she allowed herself to become dead weight and dropped steadily to the bottom of the pool. Even though it was only fourteen feet, she could feel the pain in her ears from the water pressure. She remembered what her friend Dan had taught her about holding her nose and gently blowing to equalize the pressure. She tried it a couple of times, squeezing her nose through the rubber nose guard on her mask, until suddenly her ears crackled and the pain was gone.

She looked up. Wavy images of the diving boards shimmered far above her. They looked miles away. Diane realized that she was holding her breath, even though she had scuba tanks on. She exhaled into the mouthpiece and watched the bubbles rise toward the surface. She breathed in. The air from the tank was delicious. Out. In. Out. This was fun.

Dan jumped into the pool. Diane watched his waving feet disperse her bubbles until he was standing next to her.

"Are you all right?" his eyes asked.

Diane nodded.

Diane had met Dan when she took lifesaving class during spring quarter. He was one of the lifeguards. To pass the class, each student had to jump into the pool fully dressed, drag drowning Dan over to the side, and then heft all 250 pounds of him out of the water up onto the pool deck. The first time she tried to pull him up, she went flying right over him head first into the water.

"Great lifesaver you are," he roared while the rest of the class laughed.

The second time she tried, pulling and grunting with all her ninety-pound strength, she could feel him lunging out of the water like a seal. Because of his help, she passed the class and was offered a job as lifeguard at the pool.

Both of them had come early to the pool today so that Dan could teach her how to use the tanks. They stood at the bottom of the diving pool, giggling into their masks.

Diane suddenly felt something in the water near her. Startled, she turned to find a pair of deep blue eyes staring through another diving mask into hers. They belonged to the handsome face of a guy named Johnny, a member of the university diving team. Diane had to remember to breathe again.

Diane had noticed Johnny before, during diving practice. He had blond hair, very impressive muscles, and those incredible blue eyes. She had often marveled at his grace as a diver.

The three of them stood in their diving gear on the bottom of the pool, feeling kind of silly. Then Johnny attempted a one-finger handstand on the bottom of the pool, and Diane felt compelled to imitate him. They played, doing somersaults and handstands for about thirty minutes, not even noticing when Dan left.

Finally, it was time to surface. Diane felt a flutter when, at the top, Johnny reached out to pull her effortlessly up onto the poolside. She didn't doubt that he could have pulled Big Dan out, too. He was powerfully compact and short, like a gymnast.

"You're Diane Ellingson, aren't you?" he asked as he helped her with her gear. "I saw you at the gymnastics meets this year. You're really wonderful."

The flutter was about to lift her off the ground now.

"Oh, thanks," she smiled. "I'm taking the summer off to be lazy."

"I noticed. You lifeguards really work hard," he teased. "You'd better hurry and go sit on your little chair. Guard that empty pool."

Diane grinned. It was true. The indoor natatorium pool was almost empty during the day in the summer.

The next day Johnny joined her outside during one of her breaks.

"This is the only chance I have to get a tan," she smiled at him.

"Is that why you sit and fry on that space blanket?" he asked.

"Uh huh. I've never been able to do this my whole life."

"Because of gymnastics?"

"I've always had a gym tan."

"I understand."

"I've watched you dive," Diane said. "You're super good."

"Thanks. I'm hoping to make the Olympic team someday. This year, so far, I'm ranked number ten in the nation."

"Wow. That's fantastic."

"Not good enough for the Olympics, though, but I'll get there. Listen, would you like to go out to dinner this Friday night?"

For years she had dreamed about this kind of thing. The handsome man, sunlight glinting in his blond hair, straight white teeth, blazing blue eyes. For years she had wanted to be asked to dinner on a Friday night and longed to be able to say yes. Now it was happening. She lay back on the crinkly silver blanket and allowed the sun to burn into her. She drank in the tropical aroma of tanning oil. Not for a moment did she think about playing hard to get, nor did she worry about appearing too anxious, or any of those other games. She just smiled, stretched in pure luxury, and said, "Yes! I'd love it."

"Great. I'll get your address after workout today. Do you have a favorite place you want to go?"

"No, you choose. I like anything expensive." She laughed. She had her eyes closed to the sun, but she could feel that he was smiling.

"Okay, I'll see you later. Don't get burned, now," he said, as he picked up his towel.

Diane rolled over, shaded her eyes, and watched him walk away. His wide shoulders flared out from a powerfully muscled neck. His arms hung long and muscled to his narrow waist and hips.

On Friday night Johnny picked her up in his white Ford Galaxy 500 that he called the Old White Ghost.

"It drinks more oil than gas," he told her.

He chose a moderately expensive restaurant.

When she commented on how at ease he seemed with restaurant etiquette, he said, "My stepmother is very proper.

Let me just warn you now. Don't slurp your soup in front of her, and never dangle a participle. She'll correct you."

"No, she wouldn't."

"Oh, yes she would."

"Johnny?"

"Hmm?"

"What's a participle?"

"I see that I'm going to have to whip you into shape, young lady," he smiled. "I want my family to be as impressed with you as I am."

That night at her doorstep, Johnny took her hand and gently kissed it.

"Thanks for the date."

"You're welcome," was all Diane could say. Again, this was a dream come true. He had actually kissed her hand. As he turned to walk back to his car, Diane's heart fluttered after him.

The rest of the summer and fall was consumed in the rapture of Diane's first love. For the first time in her life, gymnastics shared the glory. She was finding so much more room in her life. It was like finally throwing open the double doors to the gym to discover the endless horizon outside. Room for love. Room for school. Room to break away from family. She decided to take advantage of her scholarship to move to the dorms that fall. Johnny lived across the court from her, and they spent every extra moment together between classes and diving and gymnastics training.

Diane was in love, the kind of unworried love that allowed her to forget Johnny when she was doing gymnastics. Yet the relaxed, easier style she adapted to her workout came as a result of the happiness she felt because of him. Even when the new recruits, the hot shots, came into the gymnastics program that year, as everyone knew they would, Diane accepted without resentment that other stars might diffuse her own light. She demonstrated an attitude of caring that encompassed the whole gym, that seemed to spread through all the team members. Greg's idea of teamwork seemed to be taking shape just the way he wanted it.

If anyone suffered from Diane's happy new life-style, it was her parents. Diane's dad had always been the number-one man in her life. He missed driving her to school in the morning and picking her up in the evening. Both parents worried about Johnny. Had they taught Diane well enough to keep a clear head with him?

One night Diane and Johnny drove to a hillside viewpoint above the city to see the "submarine races."

"Submarine races? In Salt Lake?" Diane asked.

"Yes," said Johnny. "Now, watch out there. Very closely. Keep watching."

"Are they out on the Great Salt Lake?"

"Of course. Where else?"

He gently pulled her closer to his side, all the while pointing out his side of the windshield, which made her bring her face very close to his. Her hair hung long against his shoulder, crinkling with shine and smelling of perfume.

"There goes one," he said, pointing out the window. She turned, and he kissed her quickly on the lips.

"Oh, you."

"There goes another one," he said, and she turned again.

"Submarine races," she whispered. "Where did you get that one?"

"Everyone knows about the submarine races, except you, Diane."

"Then this isn't the first time you've been up here."

"Sure it is."

"Liar."

They comfortably watched the twinkling lights of the valley drift off into waves against the mountains. They talked about dreams, goals, ambitions. Johnny's fingers intertwined through Diane's. He kissed her again. His left hand slid around her waist. Diane stiffened.

Johnny pulled back, sighed, and started the car engine. "Scoot over and put your seat belt on," he said. They drove silently back to the dorms.

Some of the other divers on the team stood loitering about the door to the main lobby, and when Johnny and Diane passed by, one of the guys said, "Hey, John, I want you home and in your own beddy-bye by eleven, now."

The other guys laughed. Johnny's hand tightened around Diane's as he said, "Alvey, go give your mind a flush."

"Ooooooh," chanted the divers, laughing.

Johnny and Diane kept walking, but when he turned to her, he was shocked to see tears in her eyes.

"Hey, they were just joking," he said.

Diane shook her head but didn't say anything.

"Look, everybody knows who you are — and what you are. They know you're a good girl."

Diane looked into Johnny's eyes. He was smiling, but he wasn't mocking her.

"Don't worry," he said. "I'll take care of you."

"Okay."

He put his arm around her shoulders and held her tight.

"If you want to know the truth, every one of those guys wishes he could date you."

"Oh, sure."

"I'm not kidding. They say I'm too possessive of you."

"No, you aren't. I like it. It makes me feel like you love me."

"I'm never going to let even a snowflake come between us."

A few days later, Diane ran to the pool from workout and entered the natatorium just in time to see Johnny's last dive in the meet against Utah State. He performed a reverse two-and-a-half with a double twist off the three-meter board. Diane's spine chilled with pride.

At the end of the meet she stood waiting for him to gather his gear.

"Do you remember the first time I kissed you?" he asked. Why was he asking her that? He had just taken first place in the meet and should have had his mind full of that. Instead he was asking her about their first kiss. Diane smiled with satisfaction.

"It was on your parent's front porch after our second date," he continued. "When I was just about to kiss you, you closed your eyes and puckered up!"

"I did not."

"You did too."

Diane remembered that moment. His kiss was tender. Electrifying. The first thing her youngest sister said when Diane went into the house after was, "He kissed you, didn't he?"

"How can you tell?"

"You look stupid."

Johnny ran the towel over his hair one more time, tossed

it away into the laundry bin, and picked up his gym bag. They walked arm-in-arm into the chilly late afternoon dusk.

"You weren't the first girl I've ever kissed, you know."

"Oh, really?"

"No. I'll tell you about my first kiss if you'll tell me about yours."

"Okay."

"It was when I was twelve. I took this girl to a movie, and then when we got to her door, I said, 'Well, you know what parents do? They kiss or something.' And she said, 'Oh, yeah?' And so I puckered up and leaned toward her and she slammed the screen door on my lips."

"What?"

"Yeah! I mean, my lips were smashed in the door like this."

Johnny pushed the sides of his face together, making his lips bulge forward like a fish.

Diane giggled.

"Kithme, kithme," Johnny said as he lurched at her. She ran until he caught her and threw her, gently, to the ground. Then he kissed her softly, without the fish lips.

"Okay, now tell me about your first kiss," he said as he put his hands under her head to cushion it from the damp grass. He brushed his lips gently over her eyelids.

"No way, Jose."

"I was the first to kiss you, wasn't I? I better have been."

His lips followed the line of her jaw.

"No way," whispered Diane. "I kissed plenty of guys before you."

"Oh, yeah?"

They lay breathless in the crisp, dry leaves.

"I guess you'd never . . . ," Johnny started to say. "No. Dumb question."

He suddenly jumped up and walked her back to the dorms. Was she being a prude? She adored Johnny more than ever, but could she compromise all that she had ever believed in? Over the past months, she and Johnny had discussed many issues important to them, including religion, which naturally included her feelings against premarital sex. It was disturbing that they were so in tune on other subjects, but not on that one. Diane sighed. Being in love was sometimes terribly lonely.

Just before Christmas break, Greg Marsden paraded out the team's new leotards and warmups. His face shone with unabashed pride in his choice. Pink, with white stripes. The girls took one look and burst into loud jeers.

"They look like pajamas!"

"We won't wear them!"

Greg sulked about those uniforms through the next two months, but finally forgot his wounded pride when his team massacred the competition in their first meet of the year.

It was a good season. By the end of it, the Lady Utes had moved into fourth place in preseason standings. They were advancing on the ranks of the country's best, and Utah's media made the most of it. Diane was their favorite subject, and she was becoming a famous Utah athlete.

Near the end of the season, she started having trouble with her ankles again, but she hung on to push for the national bar title. It was not to be. At nationals she performed beautifully during team competition, but in the individual finals she fell off the bars, just as she had the year before. She also missed making All-American her sophomore year. That really hurt, because by then she knew what All-American meant. Still, she smiled. In spite of it all, because of Johnny, this had been a good, no, a great, year in her life.

Then, a few weeks later, out of the blue, Johnny told Diane, "I'm feeling too tied down by this relationship."

That night she walked around campus until the early morning hours. Finally, at three in the morning, she called Johnny's room and begged him to come over.

They met in the dorm lounge. "I can't live without you," she wept. "Don't leave me."

"I'm sorry, Diane. I don't mean to hurt you. It's just better this way."

Diane went to her room and cried the rest of the night. She walked into Greg's 7:45 A.M. sports psychology class looking more red-eyed and dejected than anyone had ever seen her.

"What's wrong with you?" Greg asked after class.

"Johnny and I broke up last night."

Greg talked with her for two hours. She told him that she had begged Johnny, she had cried, fallen apart, but it had done no good.

Finally, he asked, "Do you love him?"

"You're kidding, right?"

"And you want to stay friends with him?"

"Of course."

"If you want to stay friends, you've got to let him go. Try this. Write him a letter. Tell him you appreciate the fun times you've had together, but you respect him and his decision."

Diane did as she was coached. The next evening, she and some of the girls on the gymnastics team sat in the dorm cafeteria talking over the woes of love. Johnny sat across the room with his teammates. Diane didn't dare look over, yet she could feel his presence as if he were sitting next to her. Then one of the girls said, "I think things are looking up, Diane."

Johnny was walking toward her table.

"Are you finished eating?"

He put out his hand. He was back.

Diane, of course, was happy, but as the weeks progressed into summer, she found herself not quite so trusting of his affection. It was hard for her to let the fairy tale turn sour, but things began to change as Diane started seeing chinks in Johnny's armour. Johnny had a disconcerting, foolish streak in him, underlying that gentlemanly demeanor that she so loved.

One day when Diane was lifeguard at the pool, she looked over to see him standing at the back of the low board at the diving pool. What was he doing? The diving pool had been emptied for cleaning.

He walked out to the end of the board and started jumping, throwing his arms in wild jerks.

Diane's whole body raised in alert.

Then he squatted down like a duck, waddled off the board and over to the ladder to the high dive. He proceeded to climb to the top in a wide-legged straddle.

The young kids in her pool began to watch. Diane could hear them giggling.

Johnny waddled out to the end of the board with his hands hanging over the sides and began bounding up and down, up and down.

All the kids in her pool were watching and laughing now.

Diane sprang to her feet, horrified, as Johnny stood and bounced higher and higher.

"Get off the board!" she yelled.

"Who, me?" Johnny gestured, pointing to himself. He still bounced up and down.

Diane screamed. "Get off the board!"

Johnny pulled a hurt face. He stopped jumping, climbed slowly back down the ladder, walked past her with his head hanging and said, "Yes, ma'am."

Everyone was laughing hard now. For some reason, Diane felt foolish.

By the time their junior year started, she and Johnny were often arguing. Diane found that she resented his attempts to manipulate her. Standing in lines, he would say, "Stop twirling your hair." Or he would say, "Stand up straight. Don't arch your back like that."

And he hated the way Diane laughed.

"What's wrong with it?"

"It just sounds kind of silly."

These and other little criticisms hurt and humiliated her. The harder she tried to please him, the more he nit-picked. He told her how to dress. He spoke for her in public and coached her what to say in front of his parents until she felt frightened to open her mouth around them. She suspected that they thought she was an illiterate little fool.

Diane tried to convince herself that it wasn't worth being with someone who made her ashamed even to laugh, but there were so many times when he was the sweetest of men. He knew Diane's dreams. Diane knew that he cherished her. Finally, he talked of marriage. Diane coaxed him into taking an interpersonal relationships class with her. It broke them up for good.

After eight weeks of listening to Johnny honestly telling her how he wanted her to change, Diane balked.

"It seems like everything I do you don't like. You're trying to make me into this perfect little person that I don't like and can't be."

"I didn't realize I was doing that."

"It's asking too much for me to walk the way you want and talk the way you want. I talk good enough—and don't you tell me I talk well enough. I hate that!"

"Well, you never objected. If I told you to do something, you did it. I guess it just got out of hand."

"I wanted you to love me."

"I did. I do."

"But not enough to let me be me."

They stopped seeing each other after that. It was better to cut loose entirely. She quit her job at the pool so that she wouldn't have to pretend to ignore him during diving training.

Breaking up with Johnny opened the floodgates. Other men began pouring into Diane's life. She nearly drowned in it for a while, dating every weekend night for months. Some of the relationships lasted a few weeks, but Johnny had been her first love, and the others always proved shallow in comparison. Johnny knew what it meant to be a true athlete, and he respected the dedication that her sport required of her. She felt the others used her as an ornament. They would introduce her with, "This is Diane Ellingson, the famous gymnast."

Why can't they just say, "This is Diane, my date?" she wondered.

Again, gymnastics proved to be Diane's solace. She worked

hard. She was dedicated. There was no time to be lonely at workout, and best of all, Shannon was back, having graduated from high school. She and Diane, both grown up now, were not as close as they had been, but Diane welcomed her to the team with a feeling of relief, like finding that one missing puzzle piece.

The end of the year brought the Lady Utes to second place in the nation, just hundredths of points behind first. Diane came in fifth in the nation individually on bars, even though she again fell off in individual finals.

"Unbelievable," she said to Shannon. "I've fallen three years in a row! I'm jinxed!"

She did make All-American, though, and that made her smile to herself.

"Johnny will read it in the papers. He'll be happy for me."

Meet season was over. Diane went back to missing Johnny more than she thought possible, and missing him made her miss home. The dorms were a wilderness without Johnny's friendship. One night, she got so depressed that she threw her things into suitcases, dragged them across campus to the Union Building, put a quarter in the telephone and dialed.

"Dad? Can you come get me? I want to come home."

Chapter 10

On Sunday, May 18, 1980, a little more than a week before her twenty-first birthday, Diane wrote in her journal: "Springtime sure is lonely without a boyfriend. So many lovers walking hand in hand make me wish I had somebody." It seemed an odd entry, considering that she was once again home, surrounded by her family, and was dating numerous different men. It was more a matter of needing to feel attached, she guessed.

Two days later she wrote, "I was just sitting here wondering how things would be if I hadn't been born in this family and didn't know the people and friends I do. I wonder how much of a difference my life has made to anybody, or if it even has."

Diane realized that her years of self-serving concentration had brought her to a point of loneliness and dissatisfaction. She was suddenly tired of living for herself. She longed to relive unimportant, silly everyday moments with her brothers and sisters. Gone were the pillow fights and giggling fits as she, Marie, Louise, and Laura ran around their room, jumping from bed to bed. Her sisters were now involved with other friends and were experiencing their own struggles with work and school. Her brothers Mark and David had both married, and Grant was away at college. How she wished she could turn time back for just a week. Just a week of sitting at the table with everyone there. Diane would take notice of them. Her thoughts would be off gymnastics entirely, and she would concentrate on them.

"I never knew how important my family was to me. Help me be important to someone, someday," she silently prayed.

That summer, Diane was accepted as a counselor at Oakcrest, a youth camp designed to give twelve- and thirteen-year-old girls a week of positive, confidence-building, faith-inspiring experiences. Diane and thirty other counselors were hand picked from hundreds of applicants because of their outstanding personalities, accomplishments, and goals. During several weekend training sessions that spring, Diane learned basic camping, first aid, hiking, and outdoor survival skills that she would need as a counselor. She and the others learned songs, prepared skits, and planned themes for each of the twelve weeks of camp. When each counselor chose a nickname, Diane chose Pebbles.

Diane learned during those sessions that she was expected to put aside her own problems. She and the others were warned that they would never work harder for less tangible reward. The pay was minimal. The hours were grueling. They were expected to ignore fatigue, homesickness, and other personal concerns to devote themselves one hundred percent to the girls in their care.

Diane was ready. During the week-long precamp session at the beginning of June, she began to experience a profound change.

Oakcrest was secluded behind a brush-covered wire fence in an area of pine and aspen in the high Uintah range of the Rocky Mountains. Diane and another counselor called Woodstock shared the tiny room in the center of one of the cabins. That way each counselor would also bunk near her unit of twelve different girls each week.

The first two days were spent unpacking, planning activities, and physically setting up camp before the next week, when the first group of girls would arrive. The camp director was a young woman called Brook. She was petite and had long blond hair and deep, soft eyes. She was warm, humorous, patient, and compassionate. Diane admired her.

On the third day Brook said to the counselors, "Pick up a rock and follow me."

Diane reached for a stone about the size of her fist. "This will be easy to carry," she thought.

Brook led them to a small clearing. With a stick, she scratched in the soil two parallel lines about ten feet long and fifteen feet apart.

"You are prisoners of war and are attempting to escape. You have several obstacles to clear to gain freedom."

Diane and the others looked at one another.

"With the rocks you have gathered, you must cross this mine field, leaving no trace behind you. If anyone touches the ground, you get a strike against you. If anyone talks or laughs, that's another strike. Three strikes will result in your having to start over. This obstacle must be cleared in ten minutes, or you will have to start over."

Then she sat to the side and pulled out her watch. The counselors stood awkward and bemused. Brook was acting so strange, so militarylike and cold. Finally, one of the counselors threw her rock down on the ground and stepped on it. Another threw her rock down in front of it. The two of them held hands and tried to move forward, balancing against each other. Someone giggled.

Brook shouted, "One!"

Startled, one of the counselors standing on a rock slipped off to the ground. Brook yelled, "Two!"

"What's going on?" someone else whispered, and Brook yelled, "Three! Start over!"

By now, it was obvious to everyone that Brook was serious about this thing. It was some sort of test, and she was determined that everyone take it. Somehow, they were supposed to figure a way across the open area, working together but unable to communicate verbally. Diane suddenly realized that her small rock would be of no use to anyone, and she regretted her laziness. For the next half hour, various methods of creating a path with the stones were tried. It turned out not only to be hard work but frustrating, and in some cases, infuriating. Many of the counselors had done as Diane had and picked up small stones. When a path was finally laid, it was difficult to negotiate, and more than once, when most of them were across, someone would slip, an inadvertent word would burst out, three infractions would occur, and Brook would order the whole operation to start over. She sat there watching, completely emotionless. Finally, after nearly an hour, all thirty counselors were across the area, yet it seemed a small accomplishment for the expense in sweat and frustration.

Brook then led her counselors to another part of the forest.

For the next few hours, she put them through several more difficult tasks, each as frustrating as the first one.

During one of the exercises, after several false starts and failed attempts, Diane became upset—with the others, with the frustration of the situation, but most of all, with Brook. It was like a horrible flashback to the Academy. The intensity of the fear of Brook that overwhelmed Diane was like the fear she had sometimes felt of Michelle. Brook suddenly barked a number against Diane. Diane was sure she hadn't broken a rule but if she said anything, the whole group would have to go back. Anger tore through her, but she kept quiet. Finally they came to the final obstacle. By now, the whole group knew that cooperation was the key. As long as each person moved slowly, helping one another and staying calm, they all made it.

Then Brook led the group to a shady rock slide area where they could sit.

"What did you think of that?" she asked bluntly.

A few mumbles emerged and then a few neutral comments. Finally Diane snapped, "I hated it!"

"What did you learn from this experience?" Brook asked, her face suddenly softening at the anger in Diane's eyes. The abrupt change from hard to soft in Brook's expression made Diane realize immediately that Brook had only been playing a role. Diane was learning that she was still, after twenty-one years, setting herself up for heartbreak by putting people on pedestals, people who neither wanted nor expected her adoration.

"The only way we could get every person across was by teamwork," she said, "by helping each other no matter how hard or how frustrating."

Brook hugged Diane. Soon, everyone was hugging. They had brought each other through the obstacles and by doing so had grown to feel a deeper respect for one another, a basis for understanding, patience, compassion, and love.

"We can relate this experience to our experience with the Lord," Brook said. "Sometimes we feel alone. Sometimes life is very difficult. The Lord is always there, though, like a counselor watching over us, but he doesn't always step in to make things easier. Sometimes he sends others to help us, but most important, he allows us to make mistakes and to have the experiences that will help us grow."

Then, in a sweet, mild voice she sang a song from the movie *Pete's Dragon*:

> I'll be your candle on the water.
> My love for you will always burn.
> I know you're lost and drifting
> But the clouds are lifting,
> Don't give up — you have somewhere to turn.

Her voice drifted away into the cool afternoon breeze.

"Please forgive me for putting you through this," she said. "I can't tell you how many times I wanted to help you. But I knew you could do it. I had faith in you."

Diane sniffled, as did the twenty-nine other counselors. Arms were around her waist. Hers were linked with others. And that night when she knelt beside her bed Diane had a different image in her mind of the God to whom she prayed.

As the summer weeks went by, Diane learned what it was like to give everything she had of herself and still feel indebted for what she had received. She put her own emotional and physical needs aside as twelve giggling, emotionally charged girls took over her life each week. They drained her of sleep, ran her ragged, pumped her for advice and counsel, and teased her emotions. She had been told that for as long as they were with her, she would be a very important person to them, that what she did would help them mold their lives.

It was true. In return for what she gave, Diane received back trust. The girls idolized her. Diane saw them looking at her as she used to look at Michelle. She *could* help mold their lives. Diane vowed to do her best not to abuse that power.

On the last day of the last week of camp, after the last group of girls had left on the buses, Diane and the other counselors hung on each other and wept until they were wrung dry. It had been a summer of the deepest spiritual commitment and the most tender giving of love.

Not until she started back at the university that fall did Diane notice how changed her inner vision was. The gym, and everything associated with it, which at one time had seemed all-important, now seemed somewhat trivial. She had felt a transcendent greatness in the simple giving of oneself in service. She didn't want to lose the peace of it in frantic self-centeredness again.

"I can't believe the difference in you this year," said Greg one day. "You've come with the best attitude I've ever seen."

Diane smiled. At first, it had been the usual. Coming back from a summer off, most of the girls were overweight, out of shape, grumbling, and miserable. But during workout, while sweating through calisthenics, Diane would say, "Oooh, I love this!" When the palms of her hands rubbed off doing giants, she'd say, "This is such fun!" When her muscles felt like shredded ribbons of pain during weight training, she'd say, "I'm so happy!"

Shannon, knowing Diane was lying through her gritted teeth, laughed. Diane kept it up. "I love this. I crave this." The harder the workout, the louder she'd say it. Pretty soon, Shannon joined in, and then the others, and soon all were grunting "I love this," whining "This is great," crying "This is such fun."

The team got into shape faster than they ever had. Diane was unanimously elected co-captain of the team. It wasn't long until the initial burning and the stiff and sore aches and pains of the first couple of weeks of workout went away for the others, but Diane continued to suffer from her usual shin splint and ankle problems. She and her trainers increased therapy time before workout. She practically lived in ice at home. Finally, one day after workout, her lower back began to hurt. The next day, she could hardly walk. X-rays revealed that several of her vertebrae were compressed and inflamed, the result of an old injury. The university orthopedic doctor prescribed antiinflammatory drugs and increased ice treatments.

"But why would it be showing up now?" she asked.

"It's your age. You know, anyone else would just quit," he said to her. "But something tells me you're not one of them."

"I can't quit now, not in my last year."

"Diane, I don't know if you realize that you are one of the oldest active gymnasts in the country. Most of them burn out by eighteen. Is it any wonder?"

"Well, I've lived with pain all my life. To me, it's not worth giving up a goal. I'll be all right."

One Sunday morning just before meet season started, Diane sat in the big chair in her living room and read through her journals of the past three years. Two subjects dominated

them—gymnastics and men. She had made several attach-
ments since Johnny, but eventually the relationships had
ended. Her writings were full of a desire to be married and
have children. She came across an entry about a conversation
she'd had with her father. He had said, "Diane, you get hurt
because you're a fountain overflowing with information. You
tell everything. You have to keep some secrets. Keep the guys
wondering a little bit."

Diane had to smile. It was true. She knew that she was a
happy, fun person to be with. But she was also deeply com-
mitted to the things she most treasured in life: her faith,
gymnastics, her expectations of marriage, and her values. She
always spread out her feelings about those things early in a
relationship.

"You scare them away. They all go, 'Whoa, I don't know
if I can live up to that!' "

Diane sighed. "I don't know how to be mysterious."

As she read on through her journals, she became concerned
about her gymnastics career. So many falls, so many injuries,
so many losses colored her long career. What really bothered
her were the three falls off the bars at nationals.

She ran to the kitchen, found a pen, and sat at the table
to write.

"One thing I kept saying every year was, 'Well, I goofed
up this year but there's always next year.' Well, this is it.
There is no next year. These are the last few months of my
career as a gymnast. My first meet of the season is in five days,
and then two and a half months will race by and in April, it
will be over forever. I've been working hard, but I've got to
make every workout, every single routine count. I've got to
give 101%!"

Meet season started. The Lady Utes raced ahead from the beginning. Diane and Shannon and the others were interviewed time and again on television and radio. The Utah sports world was proud of the team's national standing, and ticket sales to gymnastics at the Special Events Center soared. Diane's personality endeared her to the crowds. Once during a meet, a little boy leaned out of the stands to ask her for her autograph. "And can I have a kiss?" he asked. Diane complied, and a photographer caught the moment.

Regionals in Albuquerque were a rout by Utah. The team swept first place, assuring them a berth at nationals, which were to be held in Utah that year. Despite the pain in her ankles, Diane had a marvelous performance in finals on the bars and came away with first place. On the dismount, however, she had twisted her foot into the mat and limped off the floor. Shannon sat down beside her when she unwrapped her ankle to check on the swelling.

"What happened, D?"

"I don't know. Shoot. Look at that."

The ankle was already turning blue.

"You'd better go get it checked."

"I will, later, after we march back out with the team."

Diane quickly rewrapped her foot.

"Why do you always use that ugly brown tape?" asked Shannon.

"I don't want anyone in the audience to see it. Nothing makes me sicker than gymnasts who go out there asking for sympathy. I don't want anyone feeling sorry for me, or thinking that I fell because I was injured."

"Is that why you cover your legs up with a towel when you ice them between events?"

"Yep."

"You don't have an image crisis, do you?"

Later, after everyone had gone home, Diane limped back into the empty gym. The lights were off. She stood there in the shadows with her hands rubbing across the top of the smooth, leather beam and thought, "I have only one more meet."

Suddenly, very tender feelings for the sport made tears come to Diane's eyes. She knew that gymnastics was ending for her. Did she have any regrets? No, she had learned so much. She was apprehensive, though. At the same time that she wanted to explore new experiences, she was scared to leave the sphere in which she had always been accepted.

She wiped tears off the top of the beam with her sleeve and left the gym.

During the next two weeks Diane's trainers tried to reduce the inflammation in her bad ankle by giving it electric galvanic stimulation treatments. She put her foot in an ice bucket that was wired to send electric current through her ankle and up into her leg. The therapy worked well. She was in good shape by the time nationals came, ready not only to perform well but to put it all away when she was finished. In the same two weeks she had made peace with her feelings and her career, deciding that there wasn't anything in life she couldn't work hard at.

Nationals. While the rest of the team members got hotel rooms in Salt Lake City, Diane slept at home in her own bed. The morning of the first day she went shopping for shoes with her sisters, and in the afternoon, her mother made her an enormous dinner of pancakes. She arrived at the training room at 5:00 P.M. for treatments. Warmup started with a thirty-minute stretch-out at 6:30. Diane's timing was on. She felt great. In the locker room the freshman gymnasts gave Diane a card that said, "Happy wishes for happy things to the best captain any team could have. We wish you success and happiness in your future." The gift was a gold heart engraved on one side with, "We love you," and on the back with, "Your '81 Fresh."

"I love you, too," Diane said. It was going to be harder to leave than she had thought.

At 8:30 the Lady Utes marched into the Special Events Center. The crowd went wild, waving red and white pompoms, screaming to the music of the pep band and the animated yelling of the cheerleaders. Diane's heart was nearly popping out of her chest.

She was first up on the vault. While she was standing at the end of the runway, a man from the top of the stands yelled, "Diane, I love you!"

Diane turned in his direction, smiled, and waved. The crowd laughed. Then she ran down the runway, did a full on, handspring off, and stuck it. Greg patted her on the back and said, "Do another one just like that." She jogged back down the runway, and halfway to the end, did a kind of leprechaun side kick. The audience clapped. Diane ran, did the same trick, and stuck it again.

"What a great start!" yelled Shannon as she hugged Diane. Utah was a full point ahead after the first event.

Utah's second event was bars. Diane knew that the team was depending on her bar score. The first three girls hit solid. The next two fell off. The pressure was on Diane, but she knew she could do it. Her mount was strong. Her routine flowed perfectly, and on the last swing into the dismount, she screamed in her mind, "I nailed my set!"

The third event, balance beam, almost took Utah from first place. Diane and two others fell off. But the last three performers had enough depth to save the team score.

Diane had a terrible warmup on floor. Her double fulls were out of control; she kept landing short and jamming her ankles. Greg became so frustrated that he swore at her. He had never sworn at her before, and she nearly came apart at that point. She was in tears when she walked out on the mat and took her beginning pose. When the double full came, she ran as hard as she could, cranked it around, landed short and stumbled out of it. She finished the routine as best she could and smiled at the cameras that followed her to the bench.

Greg came over.

"I'm sorry I swore at you, Diane. I wanted to do something to make you quit worrying about your routine, even if it meant making you mad at me."

"Greg, I wasn't pulling into myself or getting psyched out. It just wasn't there. I did my best."

"You pulled through for us on vault and bars. That's where we needed you. Look, we're about to be the 1981 national champions. Who could be sad about that?"

"Not me," smiled Diane.

The competition ended. Diane marched out on the floor with the rest of the team and accepted the thunderous applause of the audience for the number-one team in the nation. As they ran back off, Diane had tears in her eyes. No matter what happened tomorrow at individual finals, she had helped her team win the national championship. She had given her all.

Diane went into finals the next night determined that no

matter what, she was not going to fall off the bars. This time she sat on the bench next to Greg repeating over and over to herself: confidence, control, concentration.

"Stick this routine," Greg said to her as he helped set the bars while Diane adjusted the tension of the cables. The thought came to her that people had always said to her, "Don't fall off," and that's exactly what she always did. But this time Greg had said, "Stick this routine," and she knew that she would.

She chalked up her hands and started counting off her steps as the announcer said, "Next up on the unevens from the University of Utah, Diane Ellingson." She ignored the crowd as groups of people yelled, "Di-ane! Di-ane!" She waited for the judge's table to signal go with the green flag.

Confidence, control, concentration. You can do this, Di-ane. Talk your way through it.

The judges were ready. The green flag was raised. She presented herself to them by raising her arm. She clenched her fists, took a deep breath, closed her eyes, and slowly exhaled. Then she looked at the bars. She ran, mounted, and took off in the most exhilarating flight of her life. On her front somie between the bars she lost her timing for a second and was struck with horror at the possibility of falling off. But no! From somewhere, she was given the strength to muscle a kip catch out of a dead hang to make her routine look as if nothing at all had gone wrong. Triumphantly, she finished her set, sticking the dismount.

She waved to the crowd and ran to Greg who picked her up, swinging her around in a joyous hug. Over the loudspeaker came, "Ladies and gentlemen, Diane Ellingson, in the last performance of a beautiful career!"

The audience rose in a standing ovation. Diane ran out to the center of the floor and waved to the thousands of spectators, many of whom also had tears in their eyes.

A few minutes later, when the standings were posted, Diane was tied for second place.

"Diane, I'm sorry," said Greg when she ran back to hug him again.

"I don't care, Greg. I really don't. I feel like the winner because I beat the biggest mental barrier of my life. I hit my set in finals at nationals! I didn't fall off. That makes me the winner over myself!"

It was over. Diane was happy. She had triumphed over so many things in gymnastics, against so many odds—pain and discouragement being at the top of the list—to arrive in one piece at the end of her career. It felt marvelous to have done it so well. That night she slept more peacefully than she had for years.

In the next few weeks numerous radio and television stations and local newspapers spotlighted her, resurrecting her career again and again before her eyes. Then, when the fuss finally died down, a dull depression hit her. What was she really going to do next? She still had a year of studies before she could complete her teaching degree. With her scholarship used up, she needed to earn some money. She found a job as a grocery checker.

At the store she met another employee, the night manager, a young man named Bill. He was handsome, charming, and very sweet. After a few weeks of dating him, she began to wonder if she was falling in love with him. He was younger than she and still had a mission and years of school to complete before he would want to get married. In the meantime, supposing that eventually it did work out with him, how was she to direct her life?

Diane became irritable, moody, a ball of nervous energy. The only solace she found was in riding her bicycle. She would take off right after work, winding her way through the streets, up Millcreek Canyon, even as far as the university, where she would circle the HPER and get depressed again, feeling suddenly out of place there.

Finally, she realized that what was missing was the feeling she had had at Oakcrest: the unexplainable, full feeling of doing something important in the lives of others. Now she regretted having not returned there this summer, but the meager pay just wasn't enough to cover a year at the university. Next summer, though, after she graduated, she would go back. And then, on a sudden impulse, she decided that she would go on a mission. Eighteen months of that service, and by then, if Bill was still around . . .

Now the summer floated by. She and Bill saw each other daily. Was it because neither of them was pushing for a commitment that it was so comfortable?

Then one day in August the phone rang. Kurt Thomas was inviting her to join his professional gymnastics tour.

Now this, as her mother would say, was a different kettle of fish. Diane knew, even before she started adding up the obvious monetary benefits, that she would do it. The opportunity was just too wonderful. It was the rainbow's end, as far as she was concerned.

Chapter 11

Diane was waking up, although she fought like a swimmer against the current to return to the warmth that had carried her so sweetly just a few moments before. But the journey was impossibly broken up now.

"Boy," she said as she tried to roll onto her side. Oddly, her body was like lead. She lay still on her back, her eyes closed, but her skin was warm and almost liquid with comfort. A panorama of scenes from the night's dreams flashed through her brain. Why were the images of her past so much more real than this unwieldy new day?

She felt tender emotion clutching at the strands of her memory, refusing to let her go. Instances from her life shimmered in her mind, as if the images were burned into a crystal chamber of her memory. Suddenly, gratitude for her life seared into her heart. It had been so good. She was happy, like a little child garnering the opened gifts of Christmas around her for a more appreciative second look.

Eventually, the peace of her thoughts lulled her to sleep once more, where she drifted for a time. When her eyelids finally fluttered open, the dreams of the previous night were back in the recesses. The new day came on in a cold shock.

"Miss? Miss?" someone was saying.

Diane's eyes focused on a piece of paper flapping against a metal clipboard.

"Are you over twenty-one, miss?" the voice asked.

"Huh? Yeah," Diane whispered. She was aware now that people were crowded around her, quiet people in white clothing, mumbling softly to each other, to her, moving their hands rapidly over her body, behind her neck, over her face, gentle, kind, mumbling people — all except the person bobbing between them loudly asking questions.

"Do you have insurance? You'll have to sign this."

The bobbing person put a smooth white ballpoint pen in Diane's hand. It slipped between her fingers to the floor. The bobber picked it up and put it back in Diane's palm.

Diane told her fingers to take the pen, but they wouldn't, couldn't grasp it tightly. She told her arm to lift it up, and the arm obeyed, with a heavy, halting motion, but her hand dropped down like a gate swinging on a broken hinge. The pen fell to the floor again.

"Can somebody help me hold it?" Diane said.

The bobber scrambled, squeezed the pen into Diane's hand, and held it while Diane forced her arm to scribble over the paper on the clipboard.

"Oh, that's awful," said Diane. "It doesn't even look like my writing. Does it still count?"

"That will be fine," the bobber said, and she disappeared.

"Diane, I'm sorry, but we have to cut your clothes off,"

someone said. "We can try taking them off, but we risk injuring you more."

"I just bought these tights," said Diane.

"We can save them if you want."

"Go ahead," said Diane.

They cut her clothes off and quickly sponged her whole body before draping her with a hospital gown. Diane could feel that a catheter was being put in. Her first reaction was embarrassment, but she realized that if she could feel the catheter, then she probably wasn't paralyzed. She could feel the warm water, and a numbing ache in her feet and legs, and the dull probing of the doctors as they tested her reflexes. She could almost taste adrenaline pumping through her body, clearing out her mind, making it easy to smile and answer the doctor's questions, "Do you feel that? Do you feel that?" Yes, she did. A little bit.

Finally, she was being wheeled away down a long hallway. Six people lifted her onto the wide, flat X-ray table.

Her shoulder blades struck the hard surface.

"It's freezing!" she yelped.

She could feel cold air where the hospital gown had fallen askew. Then she was alone in the dark room, except for a quiet, feminine voice that came through the wall and said, "Don't move now. Hold your breath. Hold it. Hold it. Okay, let it out. Again."

The table moved back and forth, side to side, ca-ching, ca-ching, and then it stopped. By now her body had warmed the table.

Finally, the voice said, "We can't see anything."

"Oh, good," said Diane. "Maybe there's nothing wrong really. Is that good?"

"Well, it might be."

Diane lay in silence again. Her shoulder blades were screaming for release from the hard table. Diane wanted to roll just a fraction one way or the other for relief but dared not risk it.

Suddenly, a man walked into the room.

"We've got to sit you up for these X-rays," he barked.

Diane panicked.

"I can't sit up. I've injured my neck."

"Nothing shows up on the X-rays. Just sit up!"

"I can't sit up!"

Diane wanted to scream for help. Wasn't there anyone else in the room? This madman was serious and she was helpless to stop him. Where was the voice behind the wall?

"Help, oh help," she started to cry.

"Quit being such a baby," the man snapped. He struggled to get his arms into a large lead apron.

"I think I'm paralyzed," cried Diane, trying to convince him. "I can't move."

"Sit up!"

He grabbed Diane's upper arms and pulled her forward into a sitting position.

Diane screamed with pain. It felt like a knife was being shoved into the back of her neck where the biggest bone juts out.

"Ow, ow, ow, it hurts! It hurts my neck!" She was crying hysterically now while razor-sharp agony sliced through her neck and head. "I'm a certified first-aid person, and I know you shouldn't be doing this."

"Shut up."

"You're hurting me. It hurts. You can't do this."

The man was holding her forward with one hand while he fumbled with the other to move the X-ray lens into place.

"Pull your shoulders down! We can't see your neck," he snarled at Diane as he jerked her hands down into her lap.

Diane screamed again.

"I know my neck is broken," she cried. "You can't do this!"

"Take the picture!" the man shouted at the voice behind the wall.

It was over. The man laid her back on the table, stripped off the lead apron he wore, tossed it over a chair, and quickly left the room.

Diane was crying as much from anger as from pain. " 'Quit being a baby,' " she fumed. "I wasn't. He shouldn't have done that. I can't believe he did that."

Finally, a young woman came in. Diane guessed she must have belonged to the voice behind the wall. There was apologetic sympathy in her touch.

"He was out of line!" Diane sobbed.

"Shhh," the woman cooed. She tucked a heated blanket around Diane's body. Diane could feel the heat radiating to her face.

Orderlies came and rolled Diane to another room. Mike, the tour manager, was waiting there. Diane was so glad to see him. She had known him only two days, but he was beautiful. She wished he could make this shaking rage and fear of being helpless go away.

His face was twitching, his eyes filled with tears. "The doctor says it looks like you've broken your neck," he said.

It was then, right then, that she realized she could no longer feel anything. No dull aches in her legs, no cold on her skin, nothing. It had all oozed out of her body through the knife-cut canyon of pain in her neck.

"We have to call your parents."

"Oh, my gosh, don't call them. They'll die."

"We have to call them."

Diane thought about her dad. Her mom would be okay, but Dad? This would hurt him—he'd blame himself.

She was slipping into foggy darkness. A nurse called for oxygen. "Quit being such a baby!" that man had said. She wasn't a baby. She was a gymnast. She had known more pain than he could ever imagine.

Gymnastics World

Jan./Feb. 1978 $1.00

RICHARD J. INGEBRETSEN

National Junior Olympic gold medal winner

▶ All-American for three years with the University of Utah

▼ Strength and precision are the key on the beam

SCOTT LAMBSON

A perfect handstand on the high bar

Wayne and "Big D" Ellingson, 1980

Performing a giant swing on the uneven
parallel bars

Diane's mount to the bars, a straddle over the low bar

▼ With U. S. Olympian Kathy Rigby, 1979

▶ Media attention after a meet during Diane's senior year at the University of Utah, 1981

Strict concentration is required while performing on the beam
for the University of Utah

▲ Performing a beat front somersault on the uneven parallel bars

▶ A double full-twisting somersault on the floor

▼ Signing autographs for young admirers

Amazing grace—All-American gymnast, 1980

Victory! Diane's last year of
university gymnastics, 1981

Posing on the beam the morning of the accident, December 15, 1981

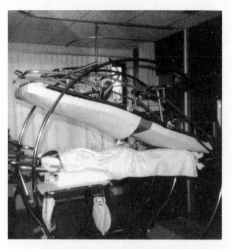

In traction on a rotating, circular-frame bed, University Doctors' Hospital, Coral Gables, Florida

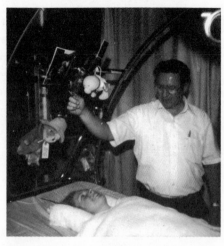

Diane's dad, Wayne Ellingson, cheers her

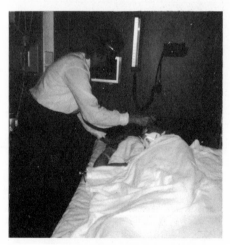

Gloria Ellingson brushes her daughter's teeth

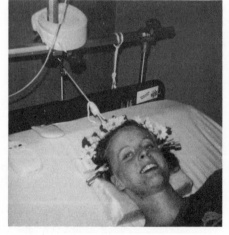

Back in Utah and in traction for the second time. Diane's mother covered the headpiece with flowers

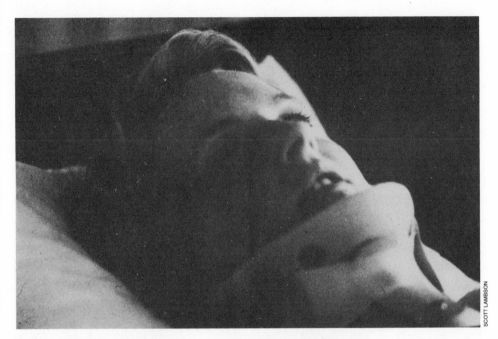

Determined, at first, to walk out of the hospital

SCOTT LAMBSON

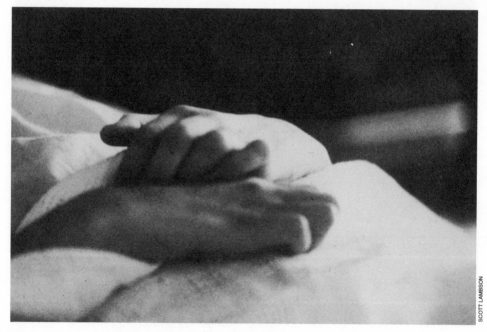

Later, conquering her useless hands became the goal

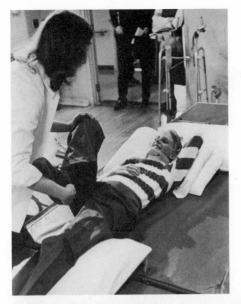

▲ Signing balloons at her first public appearance, three months after the accident, March 1982

◀ Therapy at the University of Utah Rehabilitation Center/Intermountain Spinal Cord Injury Center, 1982

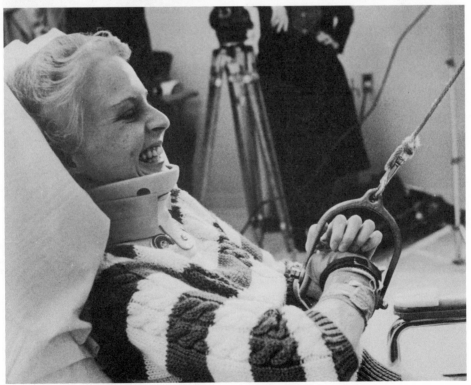

Showing off for the press—hard work pulling four pounds

Golfing great Johnny Miller and
University of Utah basketball coach
Jerry Pimm with Diane, 1982

▲ Back to classes at the University of
Utah, 1982

▶ Able to laugh again

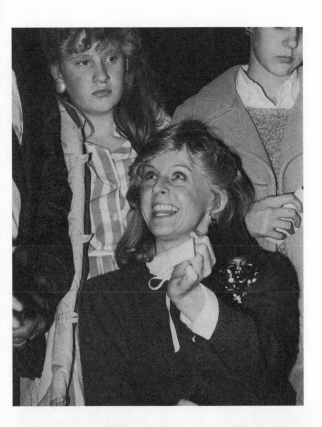

◀ Still signing autographs, now as a motivational speaker

▼ Cospeaker with Diane, Olympic gymnastics gold medalist Peter Vidmar signs his autograph for Diane's sister Laura, 1984

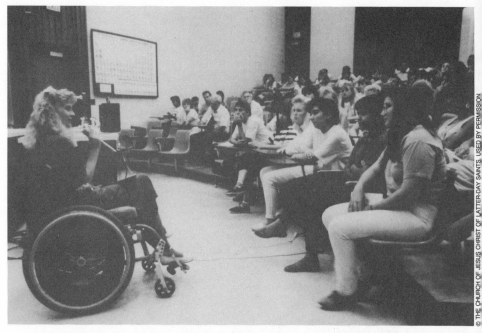

Diane admonishes her listeners to have courage and never give up

Using the CB radio in her van, equipped with hand controls and wheelchair lift

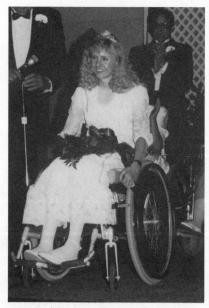

Miss Wheelchair Utah and second runner-up to Miss Wheelchair America, 1986

Teaching third grade at Rolling Meadows Elementary School, 1990

Seeing beyond the wheelchair, students at Rolling Meadows
respond to their teacher

Jackie Taylor of West Valley City hugs her favorite teacher

Chapter 12

"Mother, don't cry."

Diane's voice floated from her, jumbled and weak as if transmitted through water. Unable to anchor, protesting weakly, she drifted slowly away from her parents' touch.

What was it she remembered? Oh, yes. Other hands. Warm hands on her head, pressing lightly. Elders giving a blessing. God knew she was here.

Drifting. Floating. More hands, a horrible tugging feeling.

"Don't take my hair!"

"We have to stabilize your neck."

Too tired to struggle, she succumbed, despairing. "Not my hair."

Claws of steel were biting through the top of her head, boring into bone and grabbing hold, pulling steadily. She could hear someone saying, "It's not helping. We have to operate. Fuse C-6, C-7 together with a piece of bone from her hip. We'll do it in the morning."

Diane woke. Her parents stood above her, close, tangibly real.

"Oh," she whispered, "when did you get here?"

"Last night," said her mother. "Before surgery. You talked to us, don't you remember?"

"No. What did I say?"

" 'Mother, don't cry.' "

"I'm going to walk out of here."

"I know you will, honey."

Diane's head was clearing quickly. Light washed her eyes. She looked into her parents' faces and saw that in spite of their stoic smiles, they looked frightened, especially her father. He could not outwardly acknowledge the grief he felt for his little girl, his star.

"Dad," she beamed at him with her con artist smile, "I mean it. I'm going to walk out of here."

"I believe you will, Bi . . . honey," he said.

Diane winced. She knew that he meant to say, "I believe you will, Big D!" But he couldn't do it. She wasn't Big D anymore.

Diane spent two weeks in the hospital in Florida, long days and nights full of strangeness and pain. The first day she lay bewildered, frightened by the tubes and machines and the ungainly circular metal framework that loomed from end to end over her bed. She lay stretched out on her back with the weights of the traction steadily pulling from the top of her skull, keeping her head rigid. She couldn't feel or move anything from the chest down. A therapist came to exercise her legs to keep the hamstrings and Achilles tendons limber. He held his hands against hers and made her push or pull, exploiting what little strength she had in them. That much activity exhausted her, and she slept.

Six hours later, Gloria Ellingson entered the room to find Diane panting hysterically while the nurses fumbled with the bed.

"I'm scared," Diane cried to her mother.

Stout straps had been run across Diane's head, torso, and legs. The two nurses were frustrated, arguing with each other. "Is this what we're supposed to do?" asked one of them.

"No, do it this way," said the other.

The bed suddenly came to life. Diane's body jerked as the circular framework lurched forward and Diane was lifted to a standing position.

"I'm falling!" Diane screamed. "Help me!"

One nurse leaped to steady the motion of the bed and stopped it. Diane's eyes were wild with terror.

Her mother, hampered by the bed framework, awkwardly put her arms around her.

"It's all right, Diane. I'm holding you."

"I'm falling forward!"

"Shhh. No. No, you're not. I have you."

"I don't know where my legs are!"

Her mother turned to the nurse, "Put a strap here, across her shoulders."

"It won't make any difference."

"It will to Diane! She'll be able to *feel* the support around her shoulders."

While another strap was being tightened into place, her mother whispered soothing reassurances. Finally, it was ready.

"Are you all right, sweetheart?"

"Go ahead. I'll just think of it as a front somie." Diane was still shaking.

Diane experienced the Ferris wheel sensation of falling forward, but just as her mother predicted, the strap across her shoulders made her feel more secure. She joked, "They need Charlie's spotting belt!" She was nauseated, but the sensation abated when the bed stopped. Adjustments were made on the head strap, and she hung there, suspended, looking at the floor.

Diane was impatient from the beginning. Having to lie as if she were a corpse was terrible. Although she was paralyzed and couldn't feel anything on the outside, there was pain deep inside. Her limbs ached with agony as the muscles, toned and strengthened for many years, began to shrink, rebelling at disuse. They called it "phantom pain," and it was a nightmare to Diane.

Her parents massaged her hands and arms for hours, gently unfolding her tiny, cold fingers, bending and prodding the knuckles, stretching them out straight; but relentlessly, like frightened caterpillars, they curled tightly back under.

"My fingers look weird, Mom."

"They look fine. They're just bent."

"Do you think people will notice?"

One day early in the first week of her stay, Diane woke to an unusual calm. Minutes ticked by as she waited for someone to come into the room. The stillness seemed to intensify the painful boredom that was making the marrow of her bones crawl. She glanced over at the call button lying on the sheet next to her.

"If I can just press it with my knuckle," she whispered aloud. The button had a special soft-touch pad. Diane felt a tiny thrill of anticipation when the red light winked cheerfully on.

Several more minutes passed while Diane waited. She pressed the button again.

"What's the deal?" she thought. "I could be in here dying."

The rhythmic blipping of the heart monitor kept time with her agitation. Suddenly, a thought arrested her. Greg Marsden had taught his gymnasts that they could control their heart rates with meditation. If they needed energy, they could psyche their hearts into racing, thus pumping adrenaline into tired muscles. If they needed control, for instance, while standing on the end of the beam, they could calm their pounding heartbeats.

She experimented, concentrating on the fluorescent green blips that slowly ran across the little screen. She discovered that she really could make them change rhythm, first speed up a bit and then slow down.

"This is neat," she said to herself. She willed her heart to race. The blips moved faster and faster. She shortened her breathing to panting bursts. The blips danced jubilantly on the screen. Suddenly, the monitor belched out a strident, high-pitched alarm. Diane was so startled that her whole body seemed to jump a foot off the bed. An echo of the alarm wailed down the hall.

The door to her room burst open, and people flooded in. The resident on duty tore the covers off Diane's body and leaned in close with his stethoscope. Diane, meanwhile, was doggedly willing her heart rhythm to return to normal.

The doctor listened intently, shook his head, moved the stethoscope around to several different places on Diane's chest, and listened again. The rhythm was perfectly normal. Finally he glanced down into Diane's grinning face.

Comprehension of what Diane had done came into his face. Clearly annoyed, he snatched away the wires taped to her chest. "You obviously don't need this anymore," he said, snapping off the heart monitor and walking out of the room.

Diane couldn't help herself. A snort of laughter followed him out the door.

She slept for hours after that and woke feeling more vital. That evening she worked at moving her thumbs until she could pick up little candies by trapping them between her fingers.

Margaret was her nurse at night. Diane liked her instantly. She was big and jolly and compassionate. It was impossible for Diane to sleep suspended face down. The strap across her head needed adjusting constantly, the pain in her legs and arms was intense, her head throbbed, and she was bored to death. The nurses finally convinced Diane's parents to go back to their motel room and sleep at night. Diane missed them. From the beginning, the three of them said nightly prayers together with Dad on one side of the bed holding her hand, Mom on the other. With them close by, it was easier to fight the fear.

But Margaret made the hours bearable. She sat in Diane's room, talking to her. She brought silk from home to put under the head strap, and when that didn't work, she cut up a sheepskin for padding. It was Margaret who suggested to her parents that Diane needed to call Bill.

They moved Diane's bed to the nurses station to the phone. While she talked to him, the nurses kept watch for any doctors who might disapprove.

"Hello? Diane? You sound great!"

Diane couldn't believe how good Bill sounded. She longed for his arms around her.

"Thanks. I miss you," she said.

"I miss you too. So, when are you coming home?"

Diane wondered how much he really knew about her condition. Just what he was expecting when she did come home?

"Bill, things might not be the same."

"It doesn't matter. I love you for who you are."

"Well, I want you to know that you don't owe me anything, and I don't want you to feel that you're stuck with me if it's just too weird."

"Don't worry, I'll always be here for you."

"They shaved my hair."

"So? It doesn't matter. You'll look cute with short hair. I'll call you Butch."

Bill wrote to Diane every day. He sent her funny cards and a Ziggy doll wearing a T-shirt that said, "Guess who loves you?" In the letters were photographs of him that she hung on the bed frame.

As the days passed, Diane grew more to be the ideal patient. She maintained an impish optimism that was both charming and disconcerting. Diane's belief that she would walk out of there went beyond denial. Between forced periods of drugged sleep, she smiled, told jokes, and talked incessantly. It seemed unnatural, pathetic, like an injured dog wagging its tail after being struck by a car.

One night, when she thought she was alone during what seemed an endless torture of hanging there looking at the floor, she started to cry. Tears splashed to the cold, clean tiles below. Margaret walked in.

"What's wrong? Are you crying?"

"No."

"Yes, you are. Good!" said Margaret as she gently pressed a tissue into Diane's hand and helped her guide it to her eyes. "I'm relieved to hear it. We've all been worried about you."

Margaret soaked a washcloth with warm water.

"Here, wash your face. Need help? Good girl."

"Now, tell me about it," Margaret said.

"I'm scared," whispered Diane.

"You are?"

"Wouldn't you be?"

"I *know* I would be. I would wonder why this happened to me. Don't you feel like that, Diane? Don't you get mad?"

"No."

"Really?"

"No. It didn't *happen* to me. That's like saying I'm being punished, or something. That just couldn't be."

Margaret gently massaged Diane's shoulders.

"Why not?"

"Because I'm not bad, that's why."

Margaret smiled.

"So, what are you afraid of?"

"I don't know. I guess . . . well, what if I don't get better? What if I don't walk out of here? What if . . . "

"You go ahead and cry. That's right. Margaret's here. Let it out."

The next morning was Christmas Eve. Diane's parents sat by her side, Dad reading, Mom knitting. They fed her, fetched cranberry juice from the little refrigerator at the nurses station, and massaged her muscles until their own hands ached. Diane was in a quiet mood, so they didn't talk much.

That afternoon the gymnasts from the professional tour came to visit for the first time. It had been two weeks since the accident.

"Hi, everybody." Diane smiled.

The gymnasts mumbled subdued greetings, each dealing with his own guilty awareness that but for fate, this could be him or her. Paul Hunt and his wife, Sue, one of Diane's old Academy buddies, went to the side of the bed and kissed Diane gently on the cheek. Paul had joined the tour as a featured guest star with his gymnastic comedy routine. By now, he was becoming world famous for his antics.

"How are you?" he asked.

"Good," said Diane. She felt sorry for his awkwardness.

"Hey, what's that?" She grinned, pointing at a large package one of the others held. "A present for me?"

"Yeah."

"Oh, you shouldn't have. Give it to me!"

Everyone laughed, but they stopped when Diane was unable to grasp the package, and it fell to the floor.

"Diane, I still have to do everything for you, don't I?" said Paul.

Again, they laughed, but Paul had tears in his eyes. He picked up the package and untied the red curling ribbon.

"A bear in dancing tights!" exclaimed Diane. "How cute."

"He has a name tag. Bearishnikov."

"I love it."

Diane crisscrossed her arms around the bear. She snuggled it into her face, wishing they would all hurry and go away.

"So, when are you leaving Miami?" she asked.

"Day after tomorrow."

"Ah."

There was a long silence.

"Who did you get to take my place in the dance number?"

"I'm sure," said Sue. "Who could take your place? They just cut that part."

"They did?"

"Uh huh."

"That's nice."

Eventually they left. As soon as they were gone, Diane gave her misery free rein.

"What is it, Diane?" asked her mother as she and Dad stepped back into the room.

"Oh, I don't know. It's just Christmas, I guess. I'm feeling sorry for myself. I'm glad you're here with me, but I feel guilty that you are, too."

"Don't worry about it, sweetheart," said Diane's dad.

"I've ruined everybody's Christmas."

"No you haven't."

"Yes I have. They're going to hate me at home because you're gone."

"They'll be doing the same thing we always do every Christmas. David has invited Grant and the girls to his house for dinner tonight. They'll exchange gifts and read the Christmas story from the Bible. Then they'll go home to bed and wait for Santa to come."

"Will Santa find me here?" asked Diane.

"Dad sent him a letter first thing."

"You two," Diane said. "Come here."

That night just after midnight, Diane woke to the soft swishing sound of a large white uniform trying to sneak away.

"Get back here, Margaret. What are you up to?"

Margaret slunk back into the room.

"What's this?"

A wrapped package lay on Diane's stomach.

"Santa was just here," said Margaret. "I saw him."

"Open it. Come on. I know it was you."

Inside the box was a long, multicolored flannel nightgown trimmed with yards of lace. It buttoned up the back. How different it was from the stark white that surrounded her.

"Help me get it on."

Then Diane flopped her arms around Margaret's neck. "Oh, thank you, Margaret. I'll never forget this."

"Well, I'll never forget you, Diane. You're one brave cookie. Listen, I have another present for you. I'm not going to rotate you tonight. You get to sleep on your back."

The doctor came the day after Christmas to take the traction out of Diane's head. She lay still as ice while he unscrewed the tension. "Ow!" Diane cried as the two claws suddenly flipped out of her skull. They left two holes in the top of her head, but there was no blood. A nurse came in to wash Diane's hair. Nothing had ever felt so good, especially the gentle rubbing on her prickly scalp where her hair had been shaved.

The doctor returned to put a neck brace on Diane. She knew immediately that there were worse things than traction. It was large and bulky. Diane had visions of long-necked Ubangi women she had seen in the *National Geographic* with rows and rows of metal rings separating their heads from their bodies. The brace chafed and gouged into her chest.

"Wow, I was so excited for this," she wailed, "but I can't stand it. How am I supposed to sleep with this on?"

Margaret again made padding of sheepskin, and Diane finally succumbed to a fitful slumber that night while her father sat beside her on the bed stroking her forehead and temples.

He and her mother had refused to return to the motel with Diane in such distress.

The next day Diane was flown from Florida in a private jet to Salt Lake City and the University of Utah Rehabilitation Center/Intermountain Spinal Cord Injury Center. She cried saying good-bye to Margaret.

During the flight, Diane coaxed her mother to put her makeup on and comb her hair to cover the bald places.

"Diane, I don't know. I've never put makeup on myself, much less someone else."

"You can do it, Mom. Yesterday I threw my pillow from my chest to my knees. If I can do that, you can do this. Funny, isn't it? Two weeks ago I was doing giants on bars, and now it's a major big deal that I can throw a pillow two feet."

"Well, one thing at a time, honey," her father said.

Chapter 13

"Hey, are you famous or something?"

The copilot leaned into the cabin doorway from his seat. "The press is out there."

Diane's parents looked out. The plane had touched down, and as it slowed and turned in the direction of the terminal, they could see an ambulance parked on the tarmac. A television camera was already devouring the plane as it taxied to a stop.

"Mom, how do I look? I don't want my bald spot on television."

"I promise, it's covered up."

The doors opened. Two paramedics boarded, moved her to a gurney, and carefully lowered her from the plane to the tarmac. Diane was stunned by the familiar winter cold.

"Welcome home," said the reporter from Channel 2 television. "How're you doing?"

"Great!" Diane smiled.

"All your friends have been calling ever since the accident. They want to know how you are."

"I'm doing super. Nobody needs to worry."

Diane felt like she was going to be stepped on or tripped over, lying close to the ground on the stretcher, so it was a relief when she was lifted up into the back of the ambulance. The reporter reached his microphone in with her and asked, "When are you going to be back up on the beam?"

"Well, it might be a couple of years. Give me a little time."

The ambulance took her to the University of Utah Hospital Rehabilitation Center. Her parents met her by the elevators.

"We have to check in with admitting," her dad smiled. Everyone was smiling.

The elevator doors opened to the usual bustle of people, and then an orderly rolled Diane in and the doors shut.

"Diane?"

"Bill! I can't believe you're right here in this elevator."

Bill kissed her gently on the cheek. Diane longed to be in his arms. He held a bundle of red roses out to her.

"Diane, I'm going to keep a dozen long-stemmed red roses in your room until you get better. When these fade, I'll get some more."

"Oh, that's so sweet," said Diane, blinking back tears of frustration. What was he seeing? How did her hair look? Had he noticed her ugly hands right away?

"That's really sweet but—you know what? I like daisies better."

"Okay, I'll keep your room full of daisies."

Dear Bill. His long letters had gotten her through the last

two weeks of endless nights. What if, now that he had seen her, he grew tired of waiting for her to get well?

Diane's room was decorated with crepe paper streamers, bunches of balloons, and a sign that said, "We love you. Good luck!" This room seemed filled with hope. She was back on her own turf at her own University of Utah.

Doctor James Swenson, head of the rehabilitation center, came in. He asked her a thousand questions and poked her with a pin, asking what she could feel. That? That? He had a kindly manner about him. The nurses checked her, adjusted her catheter, and arranged her as comfortably as possible on the bed. Diane was wearing the nightgown Margaret had given her. She wanted her family to see her looking as healthy as she could look.

"Just hide that tube and that gross bag under the blanket," she said. Now she was ready. The family filed in. Bill slipped in quietly after them.

"Hi!" Diane grinned as she held her arms out. One by one they came to embrace her.

"You look great, Diane."

"We missed you."

Marie, who had hung back, finally came to Diane's bedside. Diane could see that a tidal wave of hurt was welled up behind that plaster-brave face, and she feared that Marie, who was never the faker, would let loose that pain like a flood to kill the falsely bright scene everyone, especially Diane, was fighting so hard to maintain. But Marie leaned into Diane's outstretched arms and said, "Hey, you had my name for Christmas, and I want to know where my present is."

Everyone laughed.

"Anything to get out of having to buy something," said

Diane as she tried to squeeze Marie's hand. The two of them exchanged glances. Marie's eyes said, "It's not fair, Diane." Diane's uplifted brows and crooked grin said, "I know, but I'll be okay."

They talked about Christmas and finally, when that topic drained away, Bill jumped in.

"Hey, I want to see this Ziggy haircut!"

"Oh, no, Bill."

"Aw, come on. I just want to see it."

"Well, okay, but don't laugh."

Bill lifted Diane's hair away from the shaved part of her head and rubbed his finger on it.

"Oooh, it's fuzzy. It feels good, like a caterpillar."

"Why don't we get out of here and leave these two alone for a while?" said Diane's father. Each member of her family kissed her and left.

Diane and Bill talked about his work and school and her experiences in the hospital in Florida.

"What are people saying, Bill? About me?"

"Well, most of them think you can't even talk."

"Really?"

"They think you're lying here being miserable. They have no idea that you're joking around, that kind of stuff."

Bill stood by when a nurse came in to feed Diane some soup. After she left, he said, "I wanted to come to Florida to do those things for you, Diane. I would have taken care of you."

Diane gazed into his handsome, dark brown puppy eyes.

"There wasn't much you could have done. My mom combed my hair."

"I would have done that."

"And washed my face."

"I would have done that."

"You're sweet."

"I love you."

After Bill was finally shooed out by one of the nurses, Diane lay gazing at her new surroundings. She could see brilliant pink reflecting on the snow of the mountain peaks outside her window, indicating that behind her a glorious sunset was lighting up the western sky. How exquisitely blessed she suddenly felt at that moment to have her family. To have Bill.

The next few days passed in nervous activity. News of Diane's return spread through the media. Telegrams, letters, and flowers began arriving from gymnastics teams across the country, from Greg Marsden, from other friends, relatives, and neighbors. Diane had visitors in a solid stream every evening, most of whom came dreading the sight of her broken body and spirit. Instead, they were surprised and cheered by her positive attitude.

Physical therapy began the second day. Each morning and afternoon Diane was lifted to a gurney and taken down the hall to physical therapy, where she was transferred to a thick mat. They started her with stretching exercises to keep the hamstrings in her legs limber.

"You can stretch my legs further," Diane coached the woman therapist. "Honest, I can do the splits. I can do the super splits. Push it clear to the mat."

The therapist kneaded Diane's feet back so that the Achilles tendons would not tighten up, resulting in drop foot.

After the therapist determined that Diane had full use of her biceps but limited use of her triceps, she was given weight training and pulling exercises to help strengthen her arms.

They tried putting her on a sixty-degree slant board to see if she could sit up, but having been flat on her back for three weeks, she became dizzy. They wrapped a wide, thick spandex girdle around her midriff.

"What's that for?" she asked.

"We call it a belly binder. It keeps the blood from pooling in your abdomen when you sit up. It should give you support and help with the nausea."

She also wore elastic socks to keep the blood from pooling in her legs and prevent blood clots.

The third morning, when Diane was alone in her room, she suddenly woke to the sensation that someone was pulling on her leg.

"Who's there?" she asked. As far as she could see with her limited mobility, there was no one in the room. Yet, the tugging continued.

"Is somebody in here? Who's hiding?"

She pressed the call button. When the nurse came, Diane asked if someone had been in her room.

"No, not that I know of."

"There!" said Diane when she felt the tugging again. "Someone is pulling on my leg." Panic was rising in her throat. "What's going on?"

"Oh, your leg just had a spasm, that's all."

"Wow, is that good?" Diane asked, suddenly excited that her leg moved.

The nurse hesitated. "Well, it's probably involuntary."

That evening Bill was in her room when Diane's legs suddenly spasmed violently enough to leap off the bed two or three inches at a jerk.

"My gosh, look at that!" he said. "Do you want me to go get a nurse or something?"

"No, don't bother," said Diane coolly. "They can just jump off the bed and go get her themselves."

Diane giggled. By the time the nurse came in, she and Bill were laughing hysterically while her legs continued to dance on the bed.

Diane put aside thinking about her injury as long as she was surrounded by people, but in the stillness of the night, it was easy to think. The brace made it impossible to sleep. There was no Margaret to take care of her. The nurses were too busy to cater to Diane's constant need of having to have someone adjust her neck brace. On the third night she asked the nurse to dial her mother at home.

"Mom, my neck is hurting."

"I know, honey."

"No, I mean, it's really hurting. In a different way."

"I'll be right there."

Her mother worked on the sheepskin until Diane was finally comfortable and could sleep, but when she woke the next day, the unusual pain was still there. After two more days, a specialist was called in.

"This brace doesn't fit you," he said.

"Big surprise," said Diane's mother, who was standing by frustrated. "It never did."

"It's too loose. Your neck hasn't been supported well at all."

"Isn't there something softer you can put on me?" asked Diane.

He gave her a lightweight padded collar that felt like a pillow.

"Oh, that's so much better," crooned Diane, "but my neck is still killing me."

New X-rays revealed that the bones in Diane's neck at the point of surgery had shifted almost seven millimeters.

Doctor Swenson came in the next morning.

"I hate to tell you this, Diane, but the X-rays show that your surgery didn't hold. We're going to have to put you back in traction."

Diane lay in silence, the disappointment so heavy she felt she was being crushed. A nurse came with scissors and a straight razor.

"Oh, no, don't shave more of my hair!"

"I won't take any more than is absolutely necessary, I promise."

The nurse fingered out a lock of her long hair on the left side of her head, just at the temple.

"What are you doing?" asked Diane. "Doesn't the traction go in the top of my head?"

"Not this time," said the nurse. She cut the lock of hair. Diane winced. The nurse cut the other side and soaped both areas. Diane shivered when the razor went scritch, scritch, scritch with the nightmarish tugging motions she would loathe forever. A doctor shot novocaine into both Diane's temples. Her head exploded with pain. The needle going into her skull sounded like a nail being forced through stiff Styrofoam.

"It's a good thing I'm not a swearing person," she groaned through her clenched and aching teeth.

"We have to let this sit for five minutes," the doctor said when he had finally finished.

"Okay, anything," Diane moaned. Soon, she noticed that she couldn't speak.

"I c..'. ta.k. C..'. ma.. m. m..th woo . . . oook."

"Shh," said the nurse.

Diane started to cry. It was so frightening. Her thoughts were being jumbled now, and she felt herself fragmenting into nothingness.

".m I go . . . .. be .kay?"

"Yes, yes. It's just the novocaine. I promise you'll come out of it normal."

"Pr..m.s.?"

"Diane, just stop talking. Okay?"

Now her eyes were pulling back into her head. Wind was rushing like a tornado through her ears. Diane had never known such fear. Suddenly, the paralysis of her body was nothing to this loss of herself, her being, her intellect. Please, God, she prayed. Don't let me get lost in this.

She was aware that the doctor had returned, could sense his hands on her head, and then heard but couldn't feel the metal of the traction biting through her skull. A crunching, grinding sound boomed through her as he tightened the screws into place. Immediately, a nauseating ache began to grow and throb deep in Diane's brain, deeper than the novocaine, thicker and heavier than the fog that filled her senses.

Diane was in the traction for a month this time. An arching metal bar crossed the top of her head and was screwed into her skull at the temples. A long metal cable attached to the top was stretched by heavy weights that hung off the end of the bed. The traction constantly worked loose and had to be tightened periodically, which caused Diane terrible pain and headaches that would not subside.

One advantage to this type of traction, however, was that Diane was allowed at least a little mobility from side to side.

She could lie partially propped on one side or the other for several hours at a time and did not have to hang upside down as she had done in Florida. Soon she was moved to a four-bed ward. Her roommates were a young quadriplegic named Sherry, who was paralyzed by a rare virus; a middle-aged woman named Myrna, who had caught her heel in the carpet, fallen down the stairs, and broken her neck; and a sixteen-year-old paraplegic named Madonna, whom they called Donny, who had been in a bus accident.

Diane fought to be optimistic, but misery engulfed her. The wounded areas of her scalp at the two points of traction drooled pus and fluids, which caked and had to be scraped off by the nurses with cotton swabs dipped in red Betadine. Diane cried the two or three times a day they had to do it. When someone bumped her bed she screamed in agony.

She requested that the press not have access to her. She couldn't face having the public know of her private horror. Her mother covered her head with a scarf or towel whenever anyone, including Bill, entered the room. She grinned through the pain during visiting hours as friends and family members continued to visit.

Diane was on methadone for the pain, and it made her high. She laughed and joked with her family and visitors. Then, when the drug began to wear off, she dived into sleepy depression. When the nurses turned her, she became beet red except around the eyes. She looked as if she had a skier's tan, and she joked about being on the slopes all day.

The hours oozed by like syrup. She watched television until it became abhorrent. Her parents read to her. The physical therapists came to exercise her legs and arms. Bill sat quietly holding her hands, rubbing her aching fingers and arms. Mealtimes marked the monotony.

Pain coupled with its companion, impatience, became another religion, demanding an unwilling devotion that some-times overpowered all else. Phantom pain in her legs convinced her that they were doubled up underneath her. The nurses would come to her insistent buzzing and try to convince her that they weren't.

"If I could see them, I could believe you."

"What can we do to convince you?"

"I want to see them."

Finally, an engineer attached a mirror to a bar over her bed. Diane could see her legs, and then it was easier to endure the pain spreading through her.

With the mirror above her, Diane decided she could feed herself. The occupational therapist outfitted her with a narrow Velcro cuff for her hand, which held a piece of flatware. She could see the plate in the mirror as it rested on the narrow table positioned over her chest. After hours of frustrating attempts, dropping food and spilling liquid down her neck, she finally got some nourishment to her mouth.

One day she asked a nurse to wrap her index and middle fingers together with a rubber band. She could now hold the small brushes necessary to put on her own eyeshadow, eyeliner, mascara, and blush.

She developed a high fever. Each morning at six Diane woke to the perplexed face of a lab technician who was standing with his needle poised to take blood.

"Can't find problem. Do other test," he would say in broken English.

"Why can't you just take a whole pint of blood at one

time and do all the tests? Why do you have to keep coming in here every morning?"

"Procedure. Give arm."

"Look, I keep telling you and the others that the fever is because of the traction. It was like this in Florida. As soon as it comes out, I'll be okay. I know it."

"Fever is not from traction. Something else."

"Why can't you at least take blood from my leg or somewhere that I can't feel it?"

"Arm best. Give."

Diane attended classes on various aspects of handicapped care. One day she learned that a patient has the right to refuse any treatment offered, so the next morning when the technician stood by her bedside, she said, "What do you want?"

"Must start over. Give arm."

"Look, I'm refusing your services. I want you to leave. You have nothing more to do with me."

"Must talk to Swenson."

"Good, you go talk to him. But I'm tired of being a laboratory animal!"

Impatience was overtaking Diane like a cancer. She was a prisoner in her own body, cooped up in that same ugly hospital room, slipping deeper and deeper into a depression she couldn't fight. She fretted that her friends and family would worry. People were coming to the hospital full of anxiety about her, and she felt that she had an obligation not to disappoint them. Night after night she built up a front of optimism for visitors, but the weeks of helplessness and pain had finally worn her thin. She became assertive with her nurses, demanding of their time, and critical of their work. She felt she had lost control of her life, except, she finally decided, the curtain that surrounded her bed. She had a nurse make a sign that read, "Knock before Entering," and she became very angry when people came into her space without making themselves known first.

She was frantic about her hair falling out. Not only was she not able to have it washed but now the trauma of the injury was causing it to fall out in handfuls. The nurses combed it for her, and occasionally she caught them trying to hide large wads of it as it pulled loose with the brush.

"Please be careful," she would beg.

Then one day when her mother was combing her hair, a large piece of her scalp came loose. Diane panicked.

"Oh, please help me. I have to wash my hair. It's so scummy. Mom, I can't stand it." Her mother could do nothing. Even Doctor Swenson couldn't help in this instance. The risk of infection was too great.

One morning, the nurse was called away during Diane's sponge bath. She covered Diane with a towel and stepped out. A few seconds later a hospital volunteer flipped aside her curtain.

"What do you want for lunch today?" the young man cheerfully asked.

"How dare you come in here without knocking? Get out!" screamed Diane, enraged.

The boy turned white with embarrassment and fled as Diane yelled, "Don't you ever show your face in here again. Do you hear me?"

When the nurse came back, Diane demanded to know where the sign was outside her curtain.

"Diane, there is a sign there. I'm sorry."

"It's so embarrassing. It's so degrading. I hate this place.

I can't stand being here. Nobody cares one bit about how I feel. All I am to you is a dead corpse."

The nurse leaned toward her comfortingly. Diane flung her arms around her neck and cried and cried. Diane knew she was being unfair, but she couldn't help herself. Dark, loathsome fury was crowding love and honor from her heart.

"Please help me," she begged the nurse. "I can't do this anymore. I just want to get out of here."

"I know."

Bill came later, and she complained to him. She felt guilty, knowing that she was taking him for granted, depending on his loyalty, and loving him for it. That night her parents sat with her as she cried again. Finally, it was time for them to leave, but Diane couldn't let them go peacefully. They held hands in their usual nightly prayer.

"Dear Heavenly Father, bless Diane while she is here in the hospital . . . "

"Daddy, take me home."

"Diane, Daddy can't do that. You know that," her mother whispered.

"Please, you have to take me home. I can't stand it anymore."

"There's nothing I can do," her father said, taking both her hands in his, pleading with her to understand. Diane was now begging. "I can't stay here. Please!" Finally, through her tears, she saw her father's arms reaching toward her and his agonized face begging her forgiveness as her mother dragged him from the room.

The sight struck her with pain. How cruel she had been. She lay crying with shame. A nurse came in to sit with her, to mop the tears away, and wash her face with a cool cloth.

"You will make it through this, Diane," she said. "You can do it."

Chapter 14

The despair of that night ravaged Diane like thick acid flowing through her veins. Inside her wasting flesh raged a spirit that longed to roam free among people once again, awesome with health and beauty. Dreams of when she rode her bicycle about town, singing with joyful abandon, waving to amused on-lookers, haunted her through the night and in the morning drew frustrated tears from her clenched eyes.

The only onlookers now were the visitors who came to the hospital to watch her smile and wave again. She put on a show for them, and indeed they left inspired and cheered when they had come to cheer.

But today she lay in her inescapable prison sobbing from spiritual exhaustion. She couldn't do it anymore. Couldn't face anyone else.

Her nurse, with remarkable intuition, said, "Diane, you've had enough folks in here to choke a horse. I would have gagged on it a long time ago."

"I'm just fakin' it here, aren't I?" Diane asked.

"Well, I don't know about that, but you don't have to do it, you know. People can just wait until you're feeling stronger."

"I'd rather they not see me at all than see me depressed."

"That's up to you."

From then on, visitors without previous authorization were kept from seeing Diane.

Michelle went to visit Diane one day and was unable to get past the nurses. She finally left a note and some flowers. "That's what I get for being so selfish," Diane said as tears ran down her face. "The thing I wanted most," she cried, slamming her hands down on the bed.

Then something clicked. Diane succumbed to the waste she felt her life had become. She hated everyone and everything. She threw her food trays on the floor and snapped at the nurses. Once she went into a tirade after a nurse dressed her. "You get back here and do it right! Get back here and make me look good! What do you think I am? A sack of potatoes?"

She groused at Bill and her parents in the same unfeeling way and then cried much of the time, brooding in her own self-loathing self-pity. At other times, she profusely apologized, begging their forgiveness, but within minutes was raging at them again.

"You think I should be able to just lie here and take everything. I'd like to see you do it! All I want is respect. I want to be treated like a person."

One day a therapist in a wheelchair came to see Diane. His cheerful smile made her furious, and when he started talking about her joining the wheelchair basketball team, she coldly cut him off.

"I'm not going to be in a wheelchair. I'm walking out of here, buddy. Don't even talk to me about wheelchairs. Would you mind leaving? I don't want to deal with this now."

"What a snot," Diane heard the man say to a nurse as he wheeled out the door. She was surprised to hear the nurse respond, "She'll be okay."

"Will I?" Diane thought to herself. "Oh, please Heavenly Father, will I?" she cried.

The next morning, Diane woke to the sounds of the hospital, the ding-ding-dong of signals at the nurses station, the whirring and clicking of monitors, the moaning and cries from other rooms. She could hear nurses coming and going while carrying on normal conversations about wonderful, ordinary activities that go on outside, until, listening, she nearly went crazy with a boiling unhappiness that nothing could assuage. She lay with her eyes tightly shut, praying for the peace of oblivion, when she heard someone quietly speak her name.

"Diane?"

She wouldn't answer. To answer would acknowledge existence.

"Diane? It's Brother McIntosh."

She opened her eyes. Brother McIntosh had been one of her religion instructors at the University of Utah, a man whom she admired and loved. She had unloaded her problems on him many times in the past, especially during the Johnny era. She was so glad to see him now.

"Hi," she whispered. "How did you get in here?"

Then she noticed that Brother McIntosh had someone with him, someone she recognized immediately, a very well-known leader in the Church. He took her hand in his, and Diane smiled.

"I tried to get you to speak at our youth firesides, but you wouldn't come, so I had to break my neck to meet you."

"Oh, I'm sorry," the Church leader said, his face pinched with worry.

Diane laughed. "It's a joke. I'm just kidding."

They all laughed then. Diane immediately felt a sense of ease. These men had come just at the very moment when she most needed to talk. They were immune to her venom. She could unburden her pain.

She told them how much she hated the hospital. She complained that people didn't understand what she was going through. She was weary of the responsibility of having to be strong for others, to keep from disappointing them, to fulfill everyone's expectations. At first her ire was directed at others, but it wasn't long before she addressed the real problem — her own fears. She asked if the Lord could be punishing her.

"I feel such disgust when I think of wheelchair-bound people, and quadriplegics especially. All my life, the only thing I can ever remember being afraid of was wheelchairs. I used to have bad dreams about being in one. I just feel like the only people who will be interested in me now will be weirdos and creeps."

She knew she was being ugly, repugnant, but without fear of being rejected, she told them her un-Christian thoughts and fears, anyway. "So, now, is God punishing me for my prejudice? My mom told me never to think that. I've tried so hard to be good all my life."

"You should listen to your mother. God does not inflict

unjust punishment. What you're going through, Diane, is a natural consequence of your own choices and actions."

Diane knew that this kind man, even as he spoke the difficult truth, was right. She looked over at Brother McIntosh, who had tears in his eyes. Their quiet acceptance sustained her. Somehow, they let her know that they understood her greatest fear of all, that if she ever allowed herself to get completely down, to surrender to the injury, that she would never come back up.

She felt she could say, "It's not fair," and she knew they wouldn't preach to her, yet she also knew that they understood that she wasn't indicting God. It was just a statement. Just a complaint.

"I promised myself that I would never be bitter toward Heavenly Father or the sport, either," she told them. "But it's not fair," she sobbed.

While she cried, both men, on either side of her bed, gently wiped her tears away. It felt so good to tell them everything, to have them support her as she battled her terror of losing faith. It was as if the Lord himself were holding her hands and forgiving her even as the words of fear came out of her mouth.

"Giving up isn't an option, is it? I mean, I don't really want to give up, but I don't think I can take it anymore, either."

All her words had finally flooded from her, caught in the rising tide of her tears. The two men spoke. Advocates for the Lord, they pronounced a blessing on her head. Diane felt the gentleness of their hands, and a warm feeling of peace flowed through her. Through their kindness and whispered counsel, as they filled her now-empty cup, Diane understood that the Lord was mindful of what she was going through and that he loved her with a perfect love. Her breath caught with joy when she heard, "God accepts your life, Diane, and all that you have accomplished to this point as a gift of faith. He will help you cope and give you courage and serenity that you will use to inspire others."

A brief picture of the Savior, his arms open wide with empathy, flashed through her mind as she heard the words, "Diane, when you can't go on, cast your burden on the Lord, and he will take it from you."

Diane lay quietly for a long time while her two visitors held her tiny, bent hands. Finally she said, "I'm so scared."

"You've been scared before," said Brother McIntosh. "Every time you had to learn a new skill in gymnastics; every time you faced down a new injury; whenever the doctors told you to quit. But you never gave up, Diane, and that's what made you a champion."

Diane nodded. A small ember of courage began to burn in her heart, and as it warmed through her, the cold anger that had plagued her drained away. The two men quietly slipped out of her room as Diane slept, peacefully, for the first time in weeks.

A week later, the traction was taken out of Diane's head. As soon as she was able to sit up at a sixty-degree angle, she wrote in her journal for the first time since the accident. Occasional entries had been made for her by Bill or her sisters or parents, but this night, Diane wanted to write it herself. A fine-point marker was taped to the side of her hand, and even though the words emerged shaky and slow, the feelings were clear:

"Life and my recovery are in the hands of God. I want to

walk and run and be normal again. I want to stand and face the world on my own feet. I'm so afraid of having to live my whole life in the prison of a body I can't move, on the seat of a wheelchair. At the same time, I know that I'll learn to conquer my fears. My Heavenly Father loves me and with my hand in his, I know he will be with me. My weakness will become my strength, and whether God allows me to walk again or not, I will accomplish his purpose and live a happy and fulfilling life."

Diane began to ascend rapidly out of her depression. The first thing she had to get used to was the sheer weight of her head crushing down like a cannonball on her neck. For weeks it had been stretched away from her shoulders, and now the muscles contracted in painful knots from the simple effort of holding it up. Bill massaged the kinks out of her neck before she could go to sleep. Good, dear Bill. He was still here. Diane often wondered at his patience. She knew she had been wretched to him. There were still discouraging moments, but Diane's morbidity disappeared along with the nagging fever that had plagued her during the traction. The curtain walls of her room were opened to visitors again. She patiently endured the poking and prodding of doctors, the ignominy of being dressed, the catheters, and the endless tests.

Her sense of humor returned. One day while riding on a gurney to the showers, she covered her head with the sheet as if she were a corpse. All conversation at the elevator hushed when Diane's apparently dead body was rolled up. Then, just as the doors opened, Diane flopped her arm out from under the sheet and grabbed the skirt of one of the women standing nearby.

While the subsequent scream shattered the dignified calm

of the hospital, the orderly quickly shoved Diane into the elevator and pushed the button. As the doors closed, Diane saw Doctor Swenson standing there amid the pandemonium, his knowing eyes riveted on her.

Another time, the night nurse came on her shift to find that the urine in Diane's bag was bright pink. She panicked and ran from the room to get help, thinking that Diane was bleeding to death. Doctors, nurses, and technicians were called in. Diane kept a straight face while the discovery was made that the bag was filled with cranberry juice.

As time went by, Diane and her roommates became more assertive about their wants. Myrna, the woman who had fallen down the stairs, had a C6–7 fracture like Diane. Nevertheless, she seemed to have more feeling deep in the muscles of her paralyzed body. There were nights when she lay pushing her call button, crying with pain. Diane and Donny would then turn on their call lights, too.

"They're going to come pretty soon, Myrna," Diane would say. Donny would join in. "Just try to be patient. We know you're in pain."

When the waiting became interminable, all three of them would begin yelling, "Help! Help! Help!" until the nurse would come into the room saying, "My word, don't you know what we're going through out here?" And they would say, "We don't care. Do something!"

Amazingly, two months after she entered rehab, Myrna walked out of the hospital, having suddenly regained the feeling and most of the mobility in her legs. Donny and Diane watched her go with mixed emotions. Both would have gladly traded their permanent paralysis for those few weeks of endless pain.

One day, Diane became acutely aware how really vulnerable her life was. She was alone in her room when she started to choke on a swallow of water. Try as she might, she could not summon enough diaphragm control to cough it up. She couldn't catch her breath. She was suffocating on a teaspoon of water! Finally, just when the world was turning black, a nurse came in, grabbed her, and shoved a fist under her solar plexis, causing Diane to cough up the water. Diane lay back, shaking, realizing that her life could be threatened by even the simplest functions, like taking a drink of water. She thought to herself, "Hey, I want to live! I could have died just now!"

Diane began to notice a little feeling returning to her lower rib cage, and at night she would contentedly tickle the little spot on her tummy. That one little gain gave her false hope, however, and there were days when she would lie in bed trying to force her body to come alive, to make her legs move. She would struggle violently, thrashing her arms in anger and desperation like a trapped animal.

When she was able to sit up, Diane was required to eat in the day room with the other patients. There she learned to be grateful for even her small advantages. Her appetite fell to nothing as she watched stroke victims, some with their eyes rolling in their heads, drool and slop their food all over themselves.

"There are harder things," she told herself. "Dear God, help me see my blessings."

Diane began to prepare herself mentally for the press conference that would be held in the hospital the next week, four days before NCAA Gymnastics Nationals, which was being hosted by Greg Marsden and the University of Utah.

Diane would make her first public appearance in nearly three months as a special guest at the meet. For the first time in her life, she was afraid to face television cameras. It was easy to gloat after a championship performance in gymnastics; it was another thing altogether to be seen as a broken-down derelict.

The press conference was held on March 22, 1982, in a hospital conference room big enough to accommodate the large crowd of reporters and equipment from every Salt Lake City television station, newspaper, and radio station. Diane had been one of Utah's favorite sports celebrities, and the mystery behind the past few weeks of her isolation had piqued the public's curiosity even more. Diane was thankful that Doctor Swenson was there to whitewash her period of depression with medical mumbo-jumbo. She didn't want to talk about her hopeless feelings of desperation, nor did she know how to communicate the sacredness of that day when the peaceful assurance of God's love gave her back her courage. Happily, most of the questions were about Diane's daily routine, her attitude, and her expectations for the future.

They filmed some segments of Diane in physical therapy. She was glad. Therapy had been good for her. It was not unlike the challenge of learning new tricks in gymnastics. Diane loved the physical work of it and was thrilled with her accomplishments, small as they might be. She demonstrated simple weight training and flexibility exercises, smiling all the while the cameras clicked away. The next morning, there she was beaming from the front sports page while the therapist had her leg pushed all the way up and back until her knee touched her nose. Diane was appalled that her thinning hair, which was wrapped in a loose bun on the top of her head, looked so scroungy.

That night, Bill decorated her wheelchair with red and white crepe paper and balloons and a sign that said, "GO UTES!" But he refused to go with her to the Special Events Center for the gymnastics meet.

"Why?" Diane asked. He was acting funny about this. He had been conspicuously absent during the press conference and was now very defensive.

"Look, fame and glory are your thing, Diane. You don't need me to be part of it."

"But I want you with me, Bill. I need you."

"No you don't. I don't like cameras and stuff like that."

"Is it that you don't want to be seen with me?"

Bill hesitated. "No, that's not it."

Diane felt that he did mind, and for a second, the sharpness of her shame knifed through her.

"Okay, then. I'll see you after?"

"Sure."

Diane tried to forget about Bill once she got to the sports arena. She was thinking to herself how ironic it was that her first time out of the hospital would be to this place. She had waited in this exact spot in the west tunnel at every meet for the signal to march out with her team onto the floor. Soon, now, it would be her turn to go out there alone. Over the loudspeaker she heard, "Ladies and gentlemen, please welcome back to the Special Events Center, Miss Diane Ellingson."

The instant she emerged into the light, a roar like thunder rose from the audience and in one motion every person stood up. Diane waved and smiled and tried to stop the tears as she looked up into that crowd of strangers who were giving her their hearts and best wishes. She was then wheeled over by the announcer's table where she sat for the rest of the meet. When the Utah team came out, each girl placed a dozen roses in her lap. Twelve dozen roses spilled about her chair.

That night the Lady Utes took the national championship again, for the second year in a row. Diane could hardly believe that it had been just a year since she had stood there with the team. Diane was suddenly struck with a revelation. She could let this incredible wave of jealousy sicken her, or she could get some perspective. Gymnastics had been over for her last year, anyway. So what was she planning to do now? Be a teacher. Like Jill Kinmont, the famous skier who fell during a race and ended up a quadriplegic, she, too, could be a teacher in a wheelchair. Diane suddenly grinned to herself. *The Other Side of the Mountain* had always been one of her favorite movies. Who would have thought she would turn out like Jill Kinmont? She remembered one of the scenes in the movie where Jill felt triumphant that she could pick a potato chip out of a bowl without breaking it. Diane could do that. Whatever else Jill could do, she could do it, too.

Diane threw herself even harder into physical therapy. At the beginning, she could barely lift a pound. Weeks of work yielded only minute gains, but she persisted with the same stubborn tenacity she had shown in gymnastics. Her muscles knotted and burned, but she drove them anyway. She learned to perform pressure releases, lifting herself up off the seat of her wheelchair to shift the weight from her legs and buttocks. Then she began little attempts at pushing herself in the wheelchair, which often ended in frustration. The chair was clunky and unmanageable, but Diane persisted. Her first goal was to make it from her room to the elevators. The next goal was down the elevator to the gift shop. When she finally ended up there one day, she bought herself a gift. Doctor Swenson advised her against having an electric wheelchair. The exercise of pushing herself would keep her in shape.

After being set in a sitting position on a flat surface by the therapist, Diane learned to hold herself there, a phenomenal feat considering that she had no stomach or back muscles to sustain her. She did it by pushing against her legs with her arms while balancing on her spine.

"It's too weird," she said to the physical therapist, who stood right behind her like a spotter. "I can't feel anything under me. It's like sitting in the air."

She thrashed and squirmed for days until she finally learned to roll herself over. "Just give me a doggy treat," she quipped to the therapists.

After that, she worked at getting herself up to a sitting position from lying down. Starting with a roll and then pushing against the mat with her hands and arms, elbows bent at first, inch by inch she climbed the ninety-degree angle until she sat on the narrow fence of perfect balance between falling forward and falling backward. Once there, she nudged herself back, little by little, until she leaned, gasping for breath, propped against the wall.

Competing with Donny, who was a paraplegic, Diane was determined to be first to learn to transfer from the therapy bench to a wheelchair. The moment she did it, she experienced the same elation as if she had scored a 9.5 on bars.

In occupational therapy she put puzzles together and played with blocks and paints and other such childish games, fighting depression as she watched the stroke victims and others with head injuries struggle and howl when they couldn't do any of those things. Diane rejoiced that she could manage button hooks, zipper pullers, and finger splints, and she came to appreciate the many innovations made to such simple devices as knives, scissors, and can openers to help handicapped people be self-sufficient. Her problem was, as in gymnastics, she didn't realize how fast her progress was. She expected to learn five new skills a day and got frustrated if she wasn't doing it.

When five months had passed, Diane was finally allowed to go home for a visit. It was then that she realized how fearsome life could be outside the hospital.

Chapter 15

It was Easter, a perfect time to rise from the dead of the hospital, Diane thought, as her parents wheeled her down the hallway and out of the building for her first weekend home. A couple of incidents just that morning had made escaping the place doubly desirable.

First, Diane had awakened early when the nurses' shift was changing, and as she grabbed the bars to turn herself onto her side, her legs spasmed so violently that she fell through the guard railing of the bed. She was hanging half on the floor, screaming her lungs out, and a nurse walked right by the room without even glancing in.

Donny, startled from sleep, sat up in bed with her mouth open.

"Can you believe this?" Diane wailed. The two of them broke into laughter, Diane holding on for dear life, Donny helpless to move without her wheelchair, which, according to hospital routine, had been put out into the hall for the night. All Donny could do was press the call button while rolling back and forth on her bed in hysterics.

"Shut up!" Diane shouted. "I'll end up hanging myself here!"

Finally a nurse came and pulled Diane safely back up on the bed.

Less than half an hour later, a hospital volunteer came to interview them about hospital procedures, asking them if they had any comments. Diane and Donny gave her an earful, blasting the lousy food, the lack of privacy, incompetent nurses, annoying doctors, and everything else they could think of. When they had finally spewed out all their criticism, the woman gathered her papers together and stood up.

"So," she said as she walked out the door, "I guess I can just write down, 'No complaints!' "

"This place is nuts!" Diane screamed while Donny laughed.

Now, riding in the front seat of the car alongside her dad, letting the fresh wind blow through the open window onto her face, feeling the warm spring sunshine on her arms, Diane thought how good it was to be away from the insanity of the hospital with its cold, sterile sights and smells.

The afternoon at home drifted by in happiness. Mom had baked, filling the house with an aroma deliciously familiar and welcoming. People from the neighborhood came to visit, and Diane's enthusiasm was tip-top. After a while, though, she began to feel uneasy. There always came a point in the conversation when there was nothing more to say. Diane winced at the faltering excuses as one by one, people left. Finally, she sat alone in the living room, staring at a mirror hanging on the wall. Filling the frame was an enormous wheelchair and slumped on the seat was a hunched-down, skinny, hairless freak.

Suddenly, Diane had to get away from the mirror, but try as she might, she couldn't move the heavy hospital wheelchair across the thick carpet.

"Where is everybody?" she yelled. Laura finally came, and Diane asked to be pushed into the kitchen. She talked to her mother while she prepared dinner. Other patients in rehab had come back to the hospital telling how wonderful their first visits home had been. Diane was awash with sudden guilt. She was hating this. To be in the house where she had once walked, to be unable to bound up or down the stairs at will, was like being in jail.

At dinner, they discovered that the table was too low for Diane's wheelchair.

"My food is a mile away from me," she grinned, but nobody smiled. Her dad was flitting around, nervously serving her, supervising her every move. Every few minutes someone was making adjustments for Diane, and she felt embarrassed. They were all being overly polite, not knowing what to say. Her dad cut up her food for her while everybody watched in silence. When he was finished, her dinner looked as if it had been sent through a chopper.

"Dad," Diane smiled at him, "I have teeth. I can chew. My face isn't paralyzed."

No one laughed, even though Diane thought it was kind of funny.

After dinner, Diane asked to take a shower. Her mother had been to the hospital daily for a week prior to this visit to learn how to care for Diane, and her father had installed a brand new shower chair in the tub. How good that hot shower felt. Her mother took a long time washing her hair, scrubbing her scalp with gentle, motherly tenderness.

"I love it," Diane said.

But when it was time to get out of the tub, Diane's leg bag caught on the shower chair, and the tube leading to her bladder ripped completely out of her body. Called a foli, the tube is inserted in the bladder, and then a bubble is inflated inside to keep it from slipping. That big bubble coming out panicked Diane. She threw a fit.

"Is there any blood?" she screamed, bawling. "I'm going to die. I'm going to be ruined for life. Call rehab to see if I'm going to die!"

"Goodness, Diane," her mother said, trying to remain calm. She called the hospital and was reassured that Diane was not going to die, that they merely needed to take her in to have the tube reinserted.

A while later, lying on her hospital bed, Diane was engulfed with conflicting desires. She wanted to stay here in the hospital where it was safe and ordered, where she didn't feel embarrassed about her catheters and leg bag, where taking a shower was safe, where others looked freakier than she when they ate. At the same time, she knew her mother was out in the hall waiting to take her back home.

"I just don't want to face it again," she told the nurse, but even as she spoke, she knew she couldn't hurt her mother's feelings. She allowed her mother to drive her back home.

That night, Diane sighed when she was finally situated safely in bed. "I can't feel the cool sheets against my legs," she mourned to herself. In the night she woke. The kitchen light had been on when she went to bed, casting a dim glow down the hall from her bedroom. But now, she was in total blackness. A chilling scream rose from within her. She could hear her father hit the floor in the next room, and in seconds he was kneeling beside her bed holding her tightly in his arms.

"What's wrong, honey? Shhh. Dad's here."

"Don't leave me in the dark again," Diane sobbed.

"I won't."

"I can't move. I can't see. I feel like I'm going to be attacked in the dark!"

"I'll find you a night light," she heard her mother say.

"You'll be all right," her dad promised. "I'll stay with you until you fall asleep again." When she finally woke in the morning, Easter sunshine was filling her room. Her mother dressed her for church and then wheeled her to the breakfast table. Diane laughed when she saw that it had been propped up on blocks to the right height for her. Everyone else was eating with the food right up by their faces.

"Thanks, you guys," she said.

Diane's parents had trouble getting her into the car that morning, so, when they finally entered the chapel, the meeting had started. It was the typical Diane Ellingson grand entrance.

People in the church had been praying for Diane. Primary children had written her letters and sent cards. Hours of service had been rendered to her family during the long hours and days her parents had had to be away from home to be with her. The chapel, which was full of little children, usually buzzed with subdued noise, but when Diane wheeled up the aisle, suddenly the place went silent. It was testimony meeting that day. Diane felt the expectation from the people that she would speak, so she turned to face the congregation.

"Now that I have your attention . . . " she said. Minor attempts at laughter filtered through the room. People were looking strained, as if to say, "Are we supposed to laugh?" all the while tears were running down most of their faces. Diane managed to tell the feelings of her heart. She spoke of her love and gratitude, her testimony that the Lord was with her, and then said, "I know there's a reason for all of this, and whatever happens, I'll make the best of it. Thanks for praying for me. I'm sure it has helped. Please keep it up."

Diane returned to the hospital that evening with a new perspective. The hospital was a safe zone. All her needs were taken care of. Her first taste of home life made her realize that she would have to prepare herself mentally for the next phase of her recovery, that of living disabled in an able-bodied world.

Who would be her friends? She saw well enough while she was home that the lives of her sisters, brothers, and friends in the neighborhood had run on ahead, in spite of the fact that hers had come to a dead end. Who, besides her family, would be interested in her? As if in answer, Diane received a letter from an older gentleman the next day. Inspired by an article he had read about her in the newspaper, he wrote, "You have a lot of spunk, kid, and if you ever think of adopting a grandpa, this guy's a good candidate!" On impulse, Diane wrote him back. "Sure, I'll adopt a grandpa." Now, she thought to herself, at least one friend will be waiting for me when I get out.

Diane began noticing that the standoffishness Bill had demonstrated the night she appeared at nationals was becoming a permanent shadow over their relationship. They were having conflicts over minor things. Once, his parents came to see her, arriving just at the time she had to be taken down to the showers. Bill was offended when she told them that she only had a minute to visit.

"You were rude to them!" he said to her.

"Bill, you said they were coming at 6:00, and they came at 8:30. I'm in the hospital, but I don't run the place. I had to have that shower, and your parents came late."

"If you can't accept my parents, you can't accept me."

"That isn't fair. Who said anything about you?"

Moments like that were happening often, but there were other times when Bill was a comfortable, safe part of her life. As soon as she was strong enough, he took her on excursions in her wheelchair about the hospital and grounds. They were racing along the sidewalks outside one day when they almost ran into Michelle, Charlie, and Pamela Pond, who had come for a visit. Diane rejoiced at the time that Bill was particularly charming, and she loved sharing her happiness with him later that she had finally been able to visit with Michelle.

There was a room on the fourth floor of the hospital where Diane and Bill could go to talk and usually not be disturbed. It was there a few days after she came back from her first visit home that Bill said, "Diane, you told me once that I was just infatuated with you, not in love with you. Well, maybe you were right. Maybe it's worn off or something."

Diane was horrified.

"Do you know what it's like to be in the hospital?" she demanded. "You can walk away from here every night and be with your family. You can go to work and school and see your friends. I'm a prisoner here, and don't you dare leave me! You can't do it to me yet. I can't lose you yet."

Diane was crying now. Bill lifted her from her chair and held her in his lap. He took her neck brace off and carefully leaned her head against his shoulder. A nurse came to the room to remind them that visiting hours were over, but when she saw the scene before her, she told them to take as much time as they needed.

Bill said, "I don't want to hurt you. I do love you."

Diane knew she was forcing this from him, but even with the guilt, she just couldn't let him go — not yet.

He said, "Diane, I have to have some time to myself."

"I know."

Bill was working and going to school full time, yet he had faithfully come to see her every evening since that first day more than five months before. He had been wonderful. Even when she was incoherent on drugs and in traction, he had been there. Diane knew all of this.

"I'll come once or twice a week," he said.

"All right."

Bill came every Thursday, as he promised, for the next several weeks. Then, to celebrate Diane's release from the hospital in a few days, he was granted permission to take her out to the ballet to see *Giselle*.

Diane was excited. She wore a decorative bandana over her thin hair and took her neck brace off when Bill lifted her out of the car. Bill wheeled her into the theater and lifted her into her seat. It was a clumsy, embarrassing experience for Diane. As the evening progressed, she grew more and more depressed, becoming especially obsessed with the dancers' legs. Hers had been beautiful once, but now they were emaciated, shapeless, useless traitors. Music and beauty, dance, and perfect form mocked her. When the ballet ended, Diane fought back tears and couldn't get back to the hospital fast enough. In her room, Bill gently lifted her to her bed, kissed her goodbye, and left the hospital. It was the last time Diane saw him there.

She wept that night. It was so hard for her to be in a wheelchair while everyone else was walking. In her chair she was invisible. People kept running into her. She wished Bill hadn't taken her to the ballet, of all places. How am I going to live with this all my life? she despaired. She cried herself to sleep thinking about Bill. He just can't handle it. I told him from the beginning he could leave. Oh, Bill.

Chapter 16

Being home for good was worse than Diane had thought it would be. She had psyched herself to be positive, but it was all whitewash against the dereliction her life had become. The first three months were especially difficult.

She turned twenty-three on May 27, a few days after she arrived home. People came to congratulate her but were inept at trying to make her glad that that twenty-third year had happened.

Johnny came. He stood above Diane with flowers in his hand, tanned and robust, smiling through an ugly mustache. Diane felt dwarfed and somehow shamed by his overpowering good health. She tried to cover it with a joke. "Wow, I thought I looked bad. You have more hair on your lip than I have on my head."

They talked, and as long as the conversation was about trivialities or about Johnny's training that summer with champion diver Greg Louganis, he was comfortable. Eventually, he left. Diane watched him stride down the driveway and longed, as she had done a thousand times since the accident, to leap out of that chair and run alongside him.

Bill also came. It was the first time she had seen him since the night of the ballet several weeks before. He had sent cards and letters, but they had not paved the way well for his embarrassment now. Diane felt sorry, sure that she had emotionally garroted him. She realized that she could not have had a permanent relationship with him. He was young, preparing to go on a mission for the Church, and she had already been launched into her life's mission way ahead of his schedule. She told him that and thanked him for his wonderful loyalty and compassion. She would never forget that he had been there when she needed someone most. His love had gone beyond the romantic to the Christlike.

When he kissed her good-bye, she wondered if that gentle gesture had once and for all cut her out of the mainstream of life, leaving loneliness as her only companion. Even as she remembered the tenderness of his lips, she thought of Johnny. He had been her first love. Would he be her only?

Diane slept much of the time those first three months and fainted frequently, especially if she sat up too quickly. She went back to the hospital to rehab three times a week and was making minor gains, but one of her worst fears was being realized. She had become a burden on her family, constantly in need of help to perform even the simplest tasks. Someone had to bathe and dress her, cut up her food, butter her bread, lift and carry her, fetch things, and worst of all, clean up after her when she spilled or dropped most of what she tried to pick up.

She daily struggled with impatience and would often be

driven to crying because of one thing: waiting. If she needed
something from the kitchen, she had to wait until someone
could reach it for her. She had to wait to get up in the morning,
wait to get dressed, wait to go anywhere, wait to go to bed,
wait for things, wait for people, wait, wait, wait, until waiting
became torture.

Once, when Louise was home from college and was helping
her get dressed, Diane suddenly panicked because her sleeve
got bunched up under her sweater.

"Oh, get it out! Get it out! I can't stand it! Hurry! Hurry!"

Diane was panicked, and Louise was fumbling worse because of it.

"Will you hurry up? Can't you do anything right? You're
such an airhead!"

When it was all over, and Diane calmed down, she tearfully
apologized.

"I've been so awful, Louise, and I'm sorry. You've never
said a mean thing in your life. You've always treated me like
a hero, and I am rotten to you."

Diane was often apologizing after the fact to somebody,
and she marveled at everyone's compassion. But apologies
didn't do the trick with Laura, her youngest sister. Tormenting
Diane seemed to be her favorite pastime. The scenario was
nearly always the same. Diane would need something, call
Laura who was the only child, besides Diane, still at home,
and then wait forever for a response. After a while, Diane
would call again.

"Laura!"

"What!"

"I need a drink of water, I told you."

"Okay, hang on," would come the sullen voice from the kitchen.

Minutes would drag by, but still, no Laura.

"Excuse me? About that drink of water?"

"Okay, I'll get it!"

Just when Diane was fit to kill, in would saunter Laura to plop the half-full glass of lukewarm water onto the coffee table across the room, where Diane would have to wheel over to get it. One time during this little charade, a sneer passed between the two sisters as Laura turned and walked past Diane in that infuriating teenage swagger.

"You've got the worst attitude, Laura."

"Well, you're such a snot. All you do is sit around all day."

"I'm in a wheelchair!"

"Whoopie," replied Laura.

"What is her problem?" Diane asked her mother one day, but she only got a lecture on being patient.

"Patient? What about her? What do you tell her when she's being such a witch to me?"

"I tell her to be patient, too."

Marie came from school in Idaho one weekend. She listened to Diane's complaining about Laura and then summed up the whole problem.

"She hates you right now. You've stolen her thunder, and she's ticked off at you. She's going to make you suffer for it."

Laura was thirteen, pretty, the baby of the family. Her whole life had led up to that glorious time when the other kids would be out of the house, and she could bask in the selfishness of being the only child at home. Then Diane came along and took it all away from her.

"You've got to be more patient with her, Diane."

"You sound like Mom."

"You've got to be more patient with everybody. You get so wound up when the slightest thing happens. It's your fault that you got hurt, nobody else's."

"You always say it just the way it is, don't you, Marie?"

"I try."

"I guess that's why I hate *you* so much right now."

"You love me, and you know it. I'm your best friend because I won't fall all over myself everytime you bat an eyelash, like Dad does."

"He doesn't do that."

"Oh, get real."

It was true. Concerned for Diane's well-being, he mother-henned her constantly. Laura longed for some of that attention and resented Diane because she had it.

One night Diane woke to the sound of her mother's and Laura's voices in the living room. It was strange how sometimes, since the accident, Diane's ears became ultrasensitive. On this night, she could pick up the conversation as if it were just outside her room. Laura's voice was rising in heated complaint about Diane.

"She expects me to do everything for her."

"Laura, try to imagine if you were Diane."

"I wish I was. I wish I was the one hurt! I'd love to have the whole world worry about me."

Diane was shocked. Laura was so starved for attention that she thought she'd be better off in Diane's situation! Suddenly, Diane was angry at Laura. Why did she need more attention than anyone else? How could she be so insensitive and selfish about their mother's time?

Diane wondered how her mother could do all that she did. She rose early to help Diane with bowel and bladder care, sterilize her tubes, prepare her medications, bathe, dress, and feed her. Afterwards, her mother had her normal day, performing the interminable household chores necessary for the rest of the family. To make things worse, Diane's foli leaked, and she was still having trouble regulating her diet. Sometimes her mother had to clean her up and change her clothes two or three times a day. At night, she got Diane ready and into bed. Diane never heard her complain. Now, here was Laura whining. What a selfish little brat.

The next morning, after her mother had showered and dressed her and while she was eating breakfast, Diane asked for a glass of juice. It seemed that her mother hadn't heard her because she was bustling around, gathering Diane's laundry and straightening up the room. Diane asked again.

"Just a minute, sweetheart. I want to get these clothes together to take with me."

"But I need it right now to wash down this muffin. Can't you hurry?"

"All right."

Her mother ran out, returned with the juice, and then busied herself once more draping rumpled laundry across her arm. Diane, in the meantime, drank the juice and asked her mother to come get the glass.

"Just set it on the tray."

"It gets in the way when I eat."

"Just a second."

"I can't do anything as long as I'm holding this glass. Can't you come take it now?"

Suddenly, her mother turned and said, "Oh, shut up!"

Both women were shocked. "Shut up!" was swearing, the worst thing her mother could say. Diane's eyes were round with awe. Her mother stared at her like ice. This was no slip of the tongue, no joke. She had meant it. Diane suddenly realized what a selfish brat she had been, and here she had been criticizing Laura for the same thing.

"I'm sorry, Mom," she said. The two hugged, and tears washed away the anger. Diane realized that if there was anything to learn from this, it was patience. She had never had a patient moment in her whole life.

She decided right then not to be any more of a nuisance than she had to be. She stopped asking for things unless it was absolutely necessary. Occasionally, she even skipped meals, especially loath to bother Laura.

One night, however, when her parents were out, she wished aloud that she could go downstairs to the family room to watch television.

"Why don't you?" asked Laura, in her usual snippy way.

"Because I can't get down the stairs, smarty."

"I'll carry you."

"Dad would freak. Even he won't carry me downstairs. I think he's afraid he'll fall and I'll break in half or something."

"So? He isn't here."

Laura carried Diane downstairs then and many times after that. Often they would go to Laura's room. Diane would lie on the bed, looking at Laura's yearbooks or jewelry, and they would talk about boys. They still had their tiffs, but that was better than the all-out conflict they had known before.

Diane spoke at a youth gathering only a week after coming home. Soon requests for her to speak at other functions came from all parts of the city. She accepted all that her strength would allow. She related the story of her accident and then talked honestly of her appreciation for the preservation of her life. She radiated the courage and faith of one who was determined to go on fighting despite the frightening obstacles ahead.

The most painful thing to Diane was the way her parents had started bickering over her. At one of her speeches, she looked on in amazement as her parents argued about where the slide projector and tape recorder should be set up. They were actually competing to see who could be the most helpful. Finally, Diane wheeled over to them and whispered, "Listen, I'm going to have to send you two home if you can't behave." From then on, Diane's father usually came alone to help her. It was a good niche for him. He loved being useful.

Diane's emotions were on a roller coaster. One evening she whould be giving a speech with sincere optimism and the next morning be dragging with melancholy. One day, Diane sat in front of her full-length mirror despairing. With no muscles working below her chest, she sagged in an awkward-looking slump.

"If it weren't for my backbone, I'd look like a pile of Jello," she said to herself.

That night, she dreamed that she was walking around the campus at the university frantically looking for her wheelchair. She finally found it at the bottom of the diving pool at the HPER. Diane woke, and in the dim glow of the night light reached out to touch the wheelchair by the side of her bed. How she hated it. It was disgusting to catch a glimpse of her own distorted image reflected in mirrors or store windows. Posters of her with her gymnastics teams were still on the bedroom walls. Her trophy case shimmered full against the wall. There was a picture of her on the dresser. She was standing in red warm-ups, smiling and saluting the camera with a dozen roses held out like a victory torch. Pain seared into her heart. Until that very moment, she had still nursed the sweetest hope that a miracle would happen and she would someday walk, but full realization crashed in on her.

"This isn't going to change. I'm not going to be back on the tour next year or in three years. I'm not going to be anywhere but right here. I am paralyzed."

The walls, the ceiling, the immobility of her body, and the cramped soreness of her hands closed in.

"I can't bear this anymore."

Even her tears were suffocating her. She lay weeping, far into the night, exhausted and frightened by the darkness of utter hopelessness. Finally, she prayed. "Heavenly Father, I need help. I was promised that if I came to Thee, my burden would be lifted. I know I'm never going to walk again—I'm not even asking to walk anymore. Just please help me cope. I can't stand this anymore."

In that very moment, Diane felt her despair lift from her, as tangibly as if it were being drawn away with the inhaling of God's own healing breath. Warm relief salved her burning heart. Her soul flew beyond her cramped fleshy prison, and with a prayer of thanks on her lips for the true miracle she was experiencing, she drifted into a peaceful sleep.

The next morning tranquility bathed her spirit. It was a gift of exquisite peace. She whispered her gratitude.

She felt optimistic about the day's possibilities. She asked her father to take the arms off her wheelchair, diminishing the size and bulk of it. She asked her mother to tailor her clothes to fit neatly around her tiny body, and the two of them went shopping for sweaters and overblouses that would smooth the line of her stomach, which bulged forward with the torque of her body position in the chair. If the chair was to be her constant companion, she would upstage it if she could.

That evening, Diane and her dad sat side by side reading the newspaper, she in her wheelchair, he on the end of the sofa. Suddenly, her legs went into a violent spasm that sent her flying backward. Her head smashed into the stair.

"Diane!"

"I'm okay, I guess," Diane said, shaking from the startling violence of the experience.

"You could have broken your neck!"

Diane laughed.

"Not funny, young lady. You call that doctor right now!"

The spasming in Diane's body could be controlled for the most part with medication, but not completely. She learned to recognize a maverick spasm coming on and to grab her legs to control it. Each morning, regular as clockwork, when her mother lifted her to a sitting position in bed, Diane would have one giant spasm: a violent thrust backward and then one forward.

"My jump start for the day," she joked.

Then, with her mother's help, she would bend forward slowly a number of times to work out the smaller spasms that continued in her legs. Then she sat quietly for thirty minutes after putting on a belly binder to avoid becoming dizzy. Finally, after all that, she could transfer to her chair to begin the day.

Diane got a newer, smaller, lightweight wheelchair. The insurance company authorized the building of a ramp out the back door of her parents' house, and installed an elevator from the basement to the second floor. A top floor bedroom and bath were then converted for Diane's use. By summer, Diane was able to get outside by herself and into the backyard, where she visited with her dad while he worked in the vegetable garden.

She finally met Grandpa Peterson, the man she had adopted through letters in the hospital. From then on, once a month, he took her to dinner or wherever her heart desired. Nearing seventy, he was vital, handsome, and fun. The two grew to be close friends.

Diane started dating. Young men who attended her speeches would occasionally ask her out. She would arrange to meet them at her parents' house, and then usually go on at least one date. Most of the time, she wasn't interested. In fact, all of the time, and it worried her. Since Bill, she had not been able to feel anything of the old spark that men used to ignite in her. Uncertain about her ability to love, to be a partner, she went to see her physical therapist.

"Don't make me feel stupid, but I need to know something. Do paralyzed people have sexual relationships?"

"Absolutely. There's a class offered. You can find out everything you want to know."

"Can I have children?"

"Diane, all of your internal organs function normally. It would require some very special care, but it certainly is possible."

Diane went home comforted but still troubled. She knew that she was still pretty from the neck up, especially now that her hair was growing back lush and full again, but she felt like a monster otherwise. Who could love a quad?

Summer was fully ripe now. As Diane's health improved,

she began making plans to return to the University of Utah to finish her teaching degree that fall.

Her mother drove her to the university to register. They pulled up outside the building and stopped with the car leaning slightly toward the curb. Her mother came around and opened Diane's door. At the same instant, Diane popped open her seat belt. She toppled right out onto the sidewalk.

"Hey, I saw this in a movie once," she laughed. It got even funnier as her mother struggled to get her up into her wheelchair. "This isn't funny, Diane," her mother grunted.

"I know," giggled Diane. "I'm going to have to do my own driving from now on, I can see that right now."

The next Saturday, her therapist arranged for Diane to start driving lessons in a car equipped with hand controls. She drove around the block for an hour. The next week, she was on the freeway, and the next week, she sought the approval of her insurance company to order her own van.

In the meantime, she began venturing out on longer treks in her wheelchair. It was tough going down the uneven sidewalks along her street, but each day she increased her distance by a few yards.

One day late in August, Diane followed the sounds of children playing in the school yard close to her home. The journey was long, twice what she was used to, but she persisted. She pushed for thirty seconds, rested two minutes, and pushed again. She crossed the road, but as she approached the sidewalk, the front wheels of her chair stuck in the gutter. She pushed and rocked back and forth and finally, with one heroic lurch, managed to get the front wheels up onto the curb. Now the back wheels were stuck for good, and the chair was tipping precariously backward. Time passed. The sun beat down on her head and neck, and she realized that she was about to faint. Quadriplegics don't perspire in the heat, a peculiar problem that can cause severe heat prostration. The only thing she could do was stop exerting herself and pray that she didn't faint.

A car drove down the street, and Diane waved. Whoever was driving waved back. "Oh, great," Diane thought, embarrassed. Other cars came by and did the same thing. Diane felt more like laughing than crying now. This was ludicrous.

Finally, children came pouring out of the school, but when they saw Diane trying to get their attention, they just stared as if she were some sort of monster. Diane wondered what they would do if she suddenly pitched backward out of her wheelchair onto the ground, dead. Probably run. And she wanted to be a teacher? Maybe this was an omen.

Finally, a school bus with high school kids pulled up nearby, and three boys walked toward her.

"Do you need help?" one of them asked.

"You know," said Diane, trying to appear cool, "I was just thinking I was going to spend the rest of my life in this gutter."

"Can I help you get out?"

"Oh, yes, thank you very much."

"Do you want a push somewhere?"

"No, thanks a lot," she said, smiling, wishing she could just disappear. It was not as hard going downhill to home, but by the time she sat at the bottom of the long ramp that traversed the whole length of her house, she was panting with exertion.

"Don't you think it, Diane," she said to herself. "Don't you dare give up!" Bone weary but determined, she pushed herself up the long ramp and into the house.

Chapter 17

Diane sat cradled in Marie's arms, staring at the scales as the weight indicator inched farther and farther down the numbers. Finally, it rested at 205.

"Diane, you can't keep losing weight like this. Swenson will slap you right back in the hospital."

"I know," said Diane, "but food doesn't taste good to me anymore."

Marie shrugged and stepped carefully down from the scale platform to put Diane back in her wheelchair. "Let's see. Take away my 125, you're down to eighty pounds, now. Wow!"

"Kind of ironic, isn't it? I used to starve myself to keep my weight down for gymnastics, and now I have to force myself to eat to keep my weight up."

"You make me sick."

Diane grinned as she followed Marie into the kitchen. For

once she was hungry, and she started poking around for something to eat.

Diane's life was riddled with small struggles, and there was nothing she hated worse than being stared at by people holding their breath and wondering how to help while she fumbled. Hard-to-open potato chip bags, things dropped on the floor, doors that opened inward, and turnstiles were her enemies. It was a major project to open such things as envelopes, wrappers, and soda pop cans.

While Marie discreetly looked away, pretending to search a cupboard for something, Diane picked up a plastic container from the counter and pried it open with her teeth, only to get a disgusting whiff and taste of spoiled cottage cheese. When she tried to set it back on the counter, it slipped from between her hands and spilled into her lap. She couldn't count the times something like that had happened.

Then Marie came to the rescue.

"I'm sorry."

"It's okay, Diane. Get real."

"You know, not being able to walk isn't the worst thing about this. It's my hands! I can get around in my chair, but my hands are almost useless. They make me feel claustrophobic."

"So, how are you going to take notes in class at the U?"

"I can write okay with a pen jammed between my fingers, but if I have to grab onto anything, forget it. You never know how much you use your fingers until you can't."

"Well," said Marie as she wheeled Diane back to her room to change her soiled clothing, "I suggest that you don't eat anything you can spill when you're up there. I can't be with you every minute to baby-sit, you know."

"As if you ever did anything for me, anyway."

Diane was excited about finishing her degree. The summer spent as an invalid, dependent on others, had reinforced her determination not to be a social parasite. If there was a way she could earn her own living, she would do it.

Near the end of the summer, as her strength improved, Diane ventured back into the old social structure. She returned to her sorority at school, participated in her church young adult group, and went shopping, to the movies, or to parties with old friends. There were times when she wondered if she weren't just torturing herself, sitting on the sidelines watching her friends play volleyball or softball, all the while knowing that there wasn't a fast ball she couldn't have picked out of the air, if only she wasn't paralyzed. It was impossible always to fight back tears.

Diane's first day back at the University of Utah was as grueling as any gymnastics competition. Refusing offers from her mother and sisters to come along, she had Ambucar, a chauffeur service for the handicapped, pick her up at the door of her house. Her fellow passengers were mostly old people. Diane rode in silence, feeling depressed, hoping no one she knew would see her get out of the van. Once she was on the sidewalk outside Orson Spencer Hall, though, she blanched with guilt as the old people wished her luck and waved good-bye.

"Boy, am I a snob," she said to herself. "I should be ashamed. Everyone wants respect."

Diane had wanted to go it alone from the beginning in this endeavor of going back to the university, but she underestimated the difficulty of it all.

"This is my turf!" she excitedly told herself. "I'm famous here."

She wheeled up to the building and experienced a wave of irritation when she couldn't open the door. Finally, some hurried student came by and begrudgingly held the door for her.

Once inside, she pushed herself toward the classroom. Halfway there, she grew faint. She leaned her forehead against the cool, painted cinder block wall and totally blacked out. Moments later, when she came around, the hall was empty. The muscles in her neck felt tight, and she was shaking as she pushed on. Thank goodness the classroom door was open, but more humiliation hit when she couldn't get her chair past the maze of desks.

Her entrance brought the teacher's lecture to a halt. Everyone was looking at her and she could hear, almost feel, their uncomfortable shuffling. She even caught her name as it was whispered behind someone's hand.

"Excuse me, could you help me move this desk?" she quietly asked someone.

How gagging to be in a wheelchair, she thought to herself.

When the lecture resumed, she was too spent with exhaustion and humiliation to attempt to pry her notebook out of the leather bag her father had rigged to hang on the back of her wheelchair. She sat there quaking, praying that her legs wouldn't suddenly spasm, thumping up and down with her leg bag going slosh, slosh.

Somehow, she got through that class and the next one. That night she slept as if she were back in gymnastics training. She didn't see the tears of pride shining in her mother's eyes as she undressed her nor hear her father's prayer as he held her tiny, crippled hand to his lips.

By the next morning, her neck had cramped so badly that she lay in agony, unable to get out of bed for two days. She worried that she would fall behind in school even before she started and nursed the idea of quitting, but then she told herself that quitting wasn't an option. She did decide that she was being too proud. When she went back, she asked someone for a little push down the hall. She soon discovered that asking others for help somehow closed the gap between them and the wheelchair and put them at ease. Eventually, her presence in class was no longer remarkable. Diane's wit and charm successfully upstaged her co-star, the wheelchair.

Still, to Diane, the chair remained a stigma. One day she noticed a girl walk by who had a perfect figure. Tears filled Diane's eyes. It had been so easy when her body was beautiful. That night she complained to Marie.

"Do you have any idea what it's like to be just a 'sweet spirit?' " she lamented.

The next day a friend was pushing her quickly along the sidewalk to class when they hit a shallow drainage ditch in the way. Diane went tumbling out of the chair. That same evening after a speech, a woman was helping her down the three short steps from the podium. She had the chair tipped too far back, lost her grip on the handles, and Diane fell backwards. The woman tripped and fell forward on top of her, and two girls behind her followed like a pileup in football. Three sets of squirming legs waved in the air while Diane laughed hysterically at the bottom of the heap.

The following Saturday night at a sorority activity, however, Diane felt humiliation crash in on her. She sat on the floor with pillows stuffed around her for support, eating popcorn and goodies while watching a video. She almost forgot her condition until, when the movie was over, the rest of her sorority sisters filtered out, leaving her stranded on the floor.

"I hate this!" she mourned to herself, wondering what to do. Eventually, two of her friends missed her and came back. Diane sobbed. "I hate being paralyzed!"

Her friends listened in sympathy as Diane shared long-suppressed feelings.

"Diane, you're trying too hard. Give yourself a break, will you? You expect far more from yourself than others do."

She had heard this counsel before from her coaches when she was pushing herself in gymnastics. Was it true now?

"Well, thanks for coming back for me," she said as she hugged each one. "I thought maybe a janitor would have to come along and sweep me up."

On Wednesday, December 15, 1982, one year after her accident, Diane received a note from a friend:

"Remember, in future times of bleak and gray, your life began that fateful day. It's what you make of it that sets you free!"

Diane pondered the message and wrote in her journal:

"This year has been so hard. I've been discouraged, frustrated, and depressed. Many times I've wondered how I could possibly cope. At times I have just wanted to give up, but I know that I can't do that."

A picture came to her mind, inspired by something she had read somewhere: herself, Phoenix, rising from the ashes. She had made an excellent recovery and was out of the hospital, had gotten straight A's in school, was inspiring others with her speeches and good example. Even her hair was grow-

ing longer. Wasn't that enough for a year in the life of a
quadriplegic?

Greg Marsden gave Diane four season tickets to the Lady
Utes gymnastics meets. She cheered her team on to their third
national title.

"It doesn't bother you to sit here and watch them, huh?"
asked Marie.

Before answering, Diane paused to think about her day.
She had gotten up early to attend three classes, had given a
speech at a luncheon in the afternoon, and had been up to
the Medical Center for therapy and testing. They had injected
her with dye to take pictures of her kidneys. It felt as if every
vein in her body was boiling. She got dizzy and nauseated,
and then she suddenly chilled. Then her bladder was filled
with a liquid so that more X-rays could be taken. The tests
gave her a terrible headache and tired her out, but she pulled
herself together that evening for Marie to pick her up for the
gymnastics meet. There, in spite of herself, she kept nodding
off to sleep.

"Does it bother me?" she asked Marie. "Do I wish I was
out there with them? Naw, they have to work too hard."

School ended for the year. Diane turned twenty-four.

That day she was popping wheelies around the corners of
her wheelchair ramp with her dad spotting her, just like old
times.

"Diane, the insurance company approved buying the van.
They decided it's cheaper to get you a van than pay twenty
bucks every time Ambucar has to take you somewhere."

"Great!"

When the blue Dodge van came, fully adapted with wheelchair ramp, swivel seats, and hand controls, Diane regained

some of her old freedom and a sense of control. It was equipped with an electric wheelchair lift. She learned that she had to be careful to park on the level and not back too near other cars, thus allowing room for the ramp to extend out the back. She had to plan extra time; she couldn't just jump in and out of the car anymore. Transferring from the van seat to her wheelchair and then getting to the lift and pushing the buttons to lower herself to the ground was difficult and time-consuming.

Once she was outside the van, there were other challenges to meet. The biggest problem was finding a way up and over curbs and hills, up inclined wheelchair ramps, if there were any, along broken or uneven pavement, and through heavy doors. Without gripping power in her fingers, being able only to push with the ball of her hand, she couldn't yank or twist her wheels for extra power or leverage. Even the smallest lip of cement stopped her cold. Stairs and escalators were impossible barriers. Some elevator buttons were too high or hard to push.

But with all its difficulties, the gift of independence, of being able to go out alone, made Diane feel her world expanded. How much she had taken for granted before! How measured and important each of her errands became, how welcome and appreciated each destination.

Diane wrote a letter to her insurance company to thank them for the van. She received a reply from a Mr. O'Boyle, who said, "I've never gotten a thank-you from anybody while in this business. It was really sweet of you."

One day Diane was driving along the freeway. When she tried to slow down at an exit, her hand-controlled brake wouldn't respond. Panic crept up her spine. The exit flew by.

She looked down to discover that her right leg had gone spastic and her foot was resting on the gas pedal on the floor. "Talk about lead foot," she gasped to herself as she plucked her leg away. The van slowed instantly.

She drove into the grocery store parking lot, hoping to pull into the nearest handicapped spot, but every one was occupied by cars without handicapped license plates.

"Someone probably just had to run in for a couple of things," she reasoned to herself and decided to wait. Annoyed after ten minutes, she finally drove around the lot again and took the nearest available regular space. By the time she got out of her van and wheeled over to the store, the handicapped spots were empty. A young man sauntered past and said, "Hey, lady, why didn't you park in the handicapped? If you guys aren't going to use the space, why don't they get rid of 'em and let regular folks park there?"

Diane started her last year of school that fall. She watched the hordes of healthy students scatter like ants about campus and wondered just how much time they would waste if every movement they made cost them minutes instead of seconds.

As she wheeled herself about, she began to notice individuals as they passed. She could feel pain, stress, fear, anger, or happiness emanating from them, all evident now to her. These people became her primary interest. Her school subjects, with all their theories, seemed trivial. She wanted to be out of books and into humanity. Her fireside talks became more focused on the insight others could gain for their own lives and less on making them understand about her own pain. She loosened her grip on self-pity at home and started looking for ways to ease the burdens of others. Especially her mother.

It was nearly two years now since the accident, and in that time, Diane had watched her mother age ten years.

Student teaching was coming up in the spring, and Diane knew that to be at her assigned elementary school on time, she would have to begin her day even earlier. She fretted about her mother, knowing that she needed her help and that it was exhausting her.

Diane prayed for a solution, and it wasn't long afterward that Diane's mother learned she needed an operation on her foot. It was then, when they began exploring alternatives for Diane's care during the three weeks her mother would be recuperating, that they discovered Diane's insurance would provide in-home nursing care for her for the rest of her life. She could have been using the benefit since the day she had come home from the hospital.

Diane hated the idea of a stranger taking care of her, but she quickly agreed to it for her mother's sake.

"I know I'm awful, Mom," she said, "but I don't think I could have stood it with anyone else at first. I feel really selfish, though. I think I about killed you."

"Don't be a ninny. I wouldn't have let anyone else do it, anyway."

From then on, at 5 A.M. a nurse came to help Diane with her personal care, showering, and dressing. In the evening, another nurse came to get her ready for bed.

Diane had five nurses in all, two who rotated in the morning and three who rotated at night. It was difficult for her to put her body in the hands of strangers. More than once she pondered her vulnerability and was very grateful that her nurses were both professional and modest.

The Lady Utes won their fourth national championship

that year, and Diane learned that Shannon was getting married. As happy as she was for her, she couldn't help feeling lonely herself. Pondering Shannon's marriage made her take stock of her own future. Would she have to be alone all her life? What would she do if her parents died? The thought made her ill.

"I refuse to think about it," she said to herself. "I don't think I'll live that long anyway. I really don't."

Thinking about Shannon also made her think about her old coaches, Paul and Michelle. Shortly after Paul returned from the professional tour in which she had been injured in 1981, he had a falling out with the Academy and had started his own gym. Diane saw him perform his comedy stunts every year at the U and often had the chance to talk with him.

The Ponds had carried on alone for a while but eventually moved out of state. Diane realized that she had lost track of Michelle. She feared, with great sadness, that she might never see her again. Michelle and Paul had given her a chance and for that she would be forever grateful. They had been tough at times, but from them Diane had gained a sure confidence in herself. They cheered her to struggle beyond odds when everyone else would have told her to quit.

"Michelle, I love you," Diane whispered into the darkness one night. "I wish this message could fly across the miles from my mind to yours. You'll never know how much you did for me."

Chapter 18

Diane watched twenty-five wild-eyed, unruly kids run down the hall. Five years of college had not been enough to prepare her for the student teaching experience she had been unlucky enough to draw. Half of the fourth-grade age children in her class were resource students who were one or two grades below level in ability. The regular teacher, a woman from a large Eastern city, took one look at Diane in her wheelchair and laughed.

"With kids like this, you have to be tough."

Diane tried her simple philosophy of discipline: yelling.

"Stop it!" she screamed at the kids who were running amok, but they only stopped and grinned. Diane could see in their eyes that they were thinking, "What can you do about it?"

Looking down the barrel of six weeks of Armageddon, she began to miss the peace and security of traction. Nothing she tried seemed to work. The children couldn't, or wouldn't, read. Diane tried worksheets, lectures, recitation, memorization. All of these programs were knocked out in the first round. It was a rout.

"Get back here," she yelled at four boys one day who were peeking into the women's faculty lavatory. She was trying to usher her pack of students back to the classroom from the library. Suddenly, she heard someone scream.

"There's a fire!"

She pushed her way through the mob of students jammed in the doorway of her classroom. Black, acrid-smelling smoke flowed from the top of the overhead projector at the front of her room.

"Someone pull the plug!" she yelled.

Sparks flew from the lamp box on top of the overhead projector. Diane blew the remaining smoke away, reached in with a pencil, and extracted a wad of charred yarn.

"Who put this in here?" she demanded.

Nobody, of course.

"Why do you guys have to mess everything up? Good grief!"

Meanwhile, one of the kids had run to get the principal. Diane flushed when the woman came into the room and suggested that Diane take her class back to the library until the smoke and smell could be cleared out.

Not an hour later, Diane's class started a food fight in the lunchroom. Kids were running around and food was flying overhead while Diane, exhausted from the morning's events, slept with her head on the table. In the meantime, three of Diane's kids fought out on the playground and were suspended.

The next morning Diane's cooperating teacher said, "Diane, I've been talking to the principal. Do you know you had a fire, a food fight, and three kids suspended in one day?"

Diane knew.

"Well, we've been talking, and we just don't think you can make it as a teacher."

"I'm trying!" Diane said as she struggled to hold back tears. "I just don't know what to do. Give me some help!"

"You're not doing anything wrong. It's just, well, the kids know they can take advantage of you in your condition. It's just not working for you."

"What am I supposed to do, get eaten alive here?"

"Maybe you should quit. I don't think there's any disgrace in that. Not everyone can be a teacher."

Diane was crying now. Suddenly, the bell rang and the teacher said, "Well, the kids are coming in. You'd better pull yourself together. I'll be in the library all day." She walked out of the room.

Diane pretended to search through her box of materials; all the while tears fell relentlessly. Nausea and a feeling of weightlessness began to creep over her. She took several deep breaths and finally said to herself, I'm going to get through this. The only way I'm going out of here is dead.

That afternoon, Diane's supervisor from the University of Utah walked into her classroom just at the moment when she was screaming at her kids. Diane took a ruler and smashed it as hard as she could on the desk. Instead of the resounding, authoritative CRACK! she had hoped for, it went THUNK and then bounced off the desk.

The supervisor laughed.

"That didn't work, did it?" Diane grinned sheepishly.

Later the supervisor told Diane she couldn't give her a good recommendation. "I just don't know, Diane. I have a feeling you could be a good teacher, but this class isn't working for you."

Diane was devastated. If she couldn't teach, then what could she do in life?

"Let me talk to someone," added the supervisor suddenly. "I have to see you in another situation."

Diane was given a new, smaller class for the last few weeks of student teaching. Realizing that physical threats from a wheelchair-bound quadriplegic were useless, and having had plenty of graphic experiences learning what not to do, she determined to approach this next, and last, opportunity from a different angle.

The children would respect her only if they cared about her as a person and if she respected them in return. She would reward good behavior, punish bad behavior by denying privileges, and let the students have a hand in making and enforcing the class rules.

On the first day with her new class, Diane beamed her famous smile.

"Hi," she said. "I'm Miss Ellingson. As you can see, I'm in a wheelchair. I'm paralyzed. Does anyone know what that means?" Then she held up the ring of an ordinary canning jar. "Sometimes I need help, and only my best, most special students get that privilege. Whoever earns this golden ring by good behavior gets to push me to lunch today!"

The students responded just as Diane hoped. By the time she finished her student teaching, she knew she could be a teacher. She was determined to be a great one.

She graduated from the University of Utah with her degree in teaching in June 1984. A contract with Granite School District immediately followed, but the problem was finding the right classroom situation. Her first offer was the morning half of a split session. She knew that the 7 A.M. hour would be impossible for her to make. Her second offer was a first-grade class. Visions of thirty little kids stuck in coats and boots haunted her.

"I don't do zippers!" she told the hiring supervisor.

Finally, near the end of August, she was offered a third-grade class at Rolling Meadows Elementary School in West Valley City. Two weeks before school started, Marie and some of the other teachers, who were frankly skeptical of Diane's chances to succeed, helped her set up her classroom area in the open pod system. It was one enormous warehouse of a room divided into a dozen classrooms by invisible walls. Diane asked for only two things: at least one outside wall and an overhead projector.

On the first day of school, she gathered her class on the floor about her and gave each child a slate and a piece of chalk. Then she produced the canning jar ring from among the folds of her skirt. She explained the special privilege of the golden ring of service.

Twenty-five children gazed up at their beautiful, young teacher and faced, some of them for the first time, the reality that sometimes the world is cruel, even to nice people. They asked Diane why she didn't cry because she had to sit in a wheelchair and couldn't stand at the chalkboard or walk and run at recess. They hid their own hands under their knees when they watched her funny, crooked hand draw with black marker on clear plastic overhead-projector film. The image was of a distorted spider dragging letters and numbers across the wall.

At first the children shrank back when those hands reached

out to embrace them when they came to show their work. But after a while, as they were able to look across on the same level into laughing, blue eyes, the children's fear disappeared.

Twenty-five children sat at the foot of their teacher's wheelchair, learning the ABC's and more. They were inspired and motivated. They came to realize that life is unfair, but fear is optional, and courage is more a matter of optimism than of bravado. Diane came to know that the best part of life is lived in the larger dimension of a growing, active mind.

Three years after the accident, Diane found it ironic that she was going back to rehab every few months to talk to patients who were drowning in the same mire of self-pity and hopelessness in which she had once thrashed. The scene was familiar. A child lay crying while two devastated parents sat by helpless and afraid. After three years of testing her own strength, of trying her own faith, Diane could promise them that life wasn't destroyed.

"Time really does heal wounds," she would say. "Right now you hate that wheelchair, but I promise you that one day you'll see it differently. When you've been down long enough, you'll know that the wheelchair is your best friend — your legs — your ride to wherever you want to go! The thing is, you have to decide you want to go somewhere. You'll get sick of loafing around, I guarantee you."

"Don't you ever get discouraged?" they would ask, and she'd laugh.

"Oh, yes. Look, nobody can tell you it's easy. Every day I have to psych myself up."

"Really?"

"I once threw a guy right out of my room because he wanted to talk about my options in a wheelchair."

"Wow."

"He asked me to join the wheelchair basketball team. I told him what I thought about that! He called me a snot."

"You?"

"Yeah. He knew the true me."

The word spread of Diane's dynamic talent as a speaker, and she continued to enjoy every opportunity that came her way. One evening she was a guest speaker with Darol Wagstaff, a world-champion free-style skier who, as a former drug addict, had developed a motivational seminar for youth called "A Natural High." Impressed with the poignancy of her message and the bewitching way she evoked responses from an audience, Darol asked Diane to join his organization. He offered to book her into speaking engagements on the National Motivational Speakers' circuit, and he suggested that she write a book about her life.

"Oh, brother."

"Why not? You have a lot to offer with your story. There is so much others can learn about not giving up, having courage, and going on with life."

Diane thought about that. It seemed natural, not at all extraordinary, for her to have done what she had. If not to keep going, then what? Still, she thought to herself, I wish I had known someone like me when I first got injured. It would have helped to know, in the beginning, that the terror would end, that the trauma would subside, that time would reveal alternatives and happy options. Could someone read about me and take even a little hope?

Diane worried about lacking humility, though. She loved having people surround her, giving praise and thanks. The

Bible said blessed are the meek. Writing a book seemed the essence of ego.

Yet at the same time, in a book she could express her thanks and reveal the great goodness of countless others who would otherwise go unheralded. Her mother, for one. Not a soul on earth deserved more gratitude for her service and relentless love. Diane had spent years alternately feeding and starving on her own ego only to discover the real serenity of self-worth reflected in her mother's tired, patient eyes.

Diane thought about her father. Sometime along in their travels to and from speeches, he had begun calling her "D" again. Their relationship was closer than ever. It was based on mutual respect gained through the tempering of maturity and a comfortable interdependence.

There were so many others—Miss Empey, Michelle, Paul, Greg, Nancy Theis, Johnny, Bill, Marie, Margaret, Dr. Swenson—all of whom were part of the framework around which Diane had fashioned her life.

She frowned. That was just it. The fabric seemed threadbare. She was still looking at the tangled weaving of the underside and had only an inkling of the perfectly measured, beautifully crafted design seen by the master artist. Where were the gold and silver threads? The accent, the full nap and grain of love?

"I can't write a book about my life," Diane said.

"Why not?"

"Because I'm not happy with the ending yet."

Chapter 19

Diane waved good-bye to the nurse, who was hurrying to her next appointment. The snow and icy roads of the unseasonably cold November morning had made her late, and she had barely gotten Diane out the door in time, dressed and ready for her early-morning faculty meeting.

"Are you sure you don't want me to wait until you get settled into your van?" she had asked.

"No, you just go. I'll be fine."

I should have worn my coat, Diane thought to herself as she fumbled with the switches that opened the back doors and made the wheelchair lift lower to the ground. Her teeth were already chattering. Sharp snow crystals whipped around her. But that coat is too bulky, she rationalized. It gets in the way and makes it too hard to transfer to my car seat.

She wheeled onto the ramp and nudged the switch with her knuckle. The ramp began to ascend. She hunched down into her turtleneck. Suddenly the ramp stopped halfway to the top. Diane flicked the switch, but nothing happened. She tried to make the ramp go back down. Nothing.

Diane knew instantly that she was in serious trouble. With circulation as poor as mine, she thought, I'll freeze to death! It's only 7:00. Nobody is out on a cold, dark morning like this. Oh, why did I let the nurse go?

She wanted to yell but knew the wind would only carry the sound off into black nothingness. The cold pressed in on her, making her body shudder and quake with pain. She considered throwing herself forward out of the chair but she realized that she would only smash her face into the metal floor of the van. And if she fell backward, she would topple out of the chair three feet down onto the cement driveway.

"Heavenly Father, please, help me," she prayed. "I'm so helpless here."

The cold began to cramp her jaw. She couldn't feel a thing on the outside of her body, but inside she felt the blood thickening to syrup, oozing through her veins. The cold was clogging her lungs with agony. She worried that her toes were getting frostbitten. Minutes dragged by. No cars came down the road; lights were off in the houses all around. She had no way of letting her parents know that she was just a few yards outside their safe, warm house, freezing to death.

Dad, she screamed in her brain. Dad, can you hear me? Tears formed in her eyes. Her body began to shrink into her chair. Finally, too tired to hug herself against the cold anymore, she succumbed to slumber. She imagined herself in a forest, running in panic as if lost, knowing that she was going deeper and deeper into the forest, away from the sun. Finally, she was swallowed by complete, utterly cruel, cold blackness.

"Diane? What in the world?"

Diane forced open her eyes as her father's warm hands cupped her face. Morning light filtered through the snowy air.

"Oh, Dad," she cried, trying to hold her arms out for him to lift her from the chair. "I'm so glad to see you."

"You're freezing! I came out to get the newspaper and saw your van still in the driveway. The inside lights were on. It's just a good thing I came to take a look."

Diane could hardly speak for the violent clacking of her teeth. "The lift got stuck. What time is it?"

"Eight o'clock. How long have you been out here?"

"An hour."

"Well, you foolish girl. Where's your coat?"

Her father carried her into the house to bed, where she lay for hours under a mountain of blankets, trying to get warm. She caught a cold, which eventually turned into bronchitis, complicated with a severe bladder infection. Eventually, she spent five days in the hospital with intravenous antibiotics, much of the time pondering her vulnerability.

One of the most dangerous threats to quadriplegics, once the trauma of the original spinal injury is past, is the threat of infection. Diane wondered how she would ever survive an earthquake or some other disaster, unable to get medicine or the sterile medical supplies that sustained her life. She thought of the many capable, handicapped people who could otherwise live at home but are institutionalized simply because they cannot afford daily home nursing care or the packaged, disposable, sterilized equipment required to keep themselves healthy. Diane was spending about twenty dollars a day for those things, money provided by insurance. She was so grateful.

A week later, she was once again behind the podium on

home ground at the University of Utah Special Events Center. She looked out over the audience of fifteen thousand youth who had come to hear her speak, along with Peter Vidmar, Olympic gold medal winner. She suddenly had the jitters because of the theme of the evening: "Go for the Gold!" She wondered if she deserved to be here. She had never made the grade to be in the Olympics as a gymnast, yet now, here she was on the same program with Peter Vidmar, one of the world's greatest gymnasts, who had truly earned that honor. She realized that if she hadn't been injured, she wouldn't be here at all.

"I can't tell you what a thrill it is to be able not only to compete for your country in the Olympics but to win a gold medal," Vidmar was saying. "Winning the gold—that was the most wonderful feeling I have ever had in gymnastics. I'd like for you to feel that—what it's like to be an Olympic champion—to have the whole world watching you and say, 'This guy's the best.' "

Diane cringed. How could she follow that? What could she say? I want to tell you how great it is to have *almost* made it? How great it is to be crippled for having tried?

She immediately chided herself for her negative thoughts. Peter was talking about one moment in time, one instant when others could look at you and say, "You're great." Diane knew that for her, for everybody, being worthy of the gold meant much more than that.

When the applause for Vidmar quieted, Diane slowly wheeled herself forward. The place went silent. Her tiny figure in a wheelchair, dressed in a pink sweater and skirt, was a wordless reminder of the frightening downside of the success Vidmar enjoyed. She spoke quietly.

"We were placed on earth, created in the image of God, to walk by faith. He is our Heavenly Father. We are his children. We have a divine potential. We knew it would not be easy. At times we would have to feel pain and sorrow before we could understand what true happiness and joy really are. He gave us a perspective that tells us that our life is not an accident. We have a purpose and a reason for being here."

This was a departure from Diane's usual motivational speech. Would this enormous crowd of youth sit still for a talk about spirituality? Diane hoped so, because she knew beyond doubt that her gold medal victory, as well as theirs, if it was ever to be, would be won in that realm.

"I'd like to illustrate perspective as being like a string—a long string that reaches clear across this arena. It doesn't stop there. It breaks through the walls, stretches on across the valley to the horizon, and goes to outer space. That string goes for all eternity. Somewhere in the middle of that long eternal string is one little dot—I'd say the size of a hole punch. That little dot of time is our lifetime here on earth. How we spend this hole punch of time called life will determine how we will live the rest of eternity. Do we have time to be less than our best? Do we have time to put important things aside?"

Diane looked over the crowd. She could see in their eyes that in spite of what she said, they still pitied her, that they couldn't see beyond the barrier of her paralysis. She had to let them know that she was beyond that herself.

"The scriptures teach us that God's children will be resurrected. That means we will receive a perfect body for the rest of eternity. That knowledge is very comforting to me because I know that life is short and eternity is long. This wheelchair is no big deal because I know that very soon, I'll stand. I'll walk. I'll run. I'll dance. And I'll tumble. I only hope that each one of us will find it important enough to make ourselves as clean, as pure, and as perfect on the inside as we will be one day on the outside, so that when we meet our Savior, it will be a great and glorious day, and he will say to us, 'Well done, thou good and faithful servant: . . . enter thou into the joy of thy lord.' " (Matthew 25:21.)

Diane was amazed at the strength of her own conviction. She had come a very long way since those days of desperation in the hospital after her injury. Today, she understood a little bit better what the Lord meant when he said that by grace, we are saved. Grace was a state of understanding the eternal nature of oneself.

Suddenly, she knew that she had to call Michelle. The next day, by contacting friends and gymnastics associations, she finally located Michelle's phone number in California. Just as she suspected, Michelle not only grieved for Diane's injury but carried a huge burden of guilt besides.

"Diane, I worry that all you remember was that I was a horrible person."

"No, I don't."

"I did make a lot of mistakes. I was way too hard on you and Shannon. It was like having a first child—I experimented on you. I do things differently now."

Diane's heart was bursting. "You were really hard, but I learned from you that you just can't give up. I would never have reached my potential otherwise. I idolized you."

"I know. It was hard to live up to what you thought of me. It was more of a burden than anything else. I hated it."

Diane flinched. "I'm sorry, Michelle. Even if I had known

how you felt, I don't think I could have loved you less. You
were the key to my dreams."

"I wonder."

"That's why I called you, Michelle. I want you to know
that I think God put us together at a certain time and place
because he knew you were the one to prepare me for my life
now. Every minute and hour I spent in that hospital, sweating
my guts out in therapy, crying my eyes out alone in the dark,
I could see and hear you coaching me. I needed somebody
tough so I could be tough on myself. I want you to know that.
You made all the difference in my life."

Michelle finally spoke. "I don't know what to say, Diane.
I'm glad you called."

"Just say you believe me, Michelle."

"Okay."

"And don't worry anymore. I'm fine. I really am."

"You were always fine, Diane. Really fine."

A few days after Christmas that year, the phone rang.
Another young man wanted to date her after hearing her speak.
As usual, she arranged to meet him in her parents' living
room. This one impressed her more than most, however, not
only because he was six feet tall and had blond hair and blue
eyes, but because he seemed to be more interested in her than
in himself. Many of the men who called Diane were emotionally and spiritually weak, and they saw in her someone
who could motivate and encourage them. Steve, on the other
hand, didn't seem to need confidence. He was a licensed
practical nurse and a student of physical therapy. His warmth,
cheerfulness, and attentiveness left little doubt that he was
attracted to Diane. For the first time in two years, she felt the
old flutter. She was elated.

"What do you do in your spare time?" Steve asked her.

"Well . . . "

"What did you used to do?"

"Oh, baseball, hiking, camping, and fishing with my family. I don't know. I never really had any spare time."

"Have you done any of that since?"

"No."

"Well, it's about time you did."

Steve changed Diane's life. That winter he took her sledding and introduced her to skiing through a friend in Park City who taught handicapped people to ski in a special toboggan. It wasn't an enjoyable experience for her, though, especially when she lost control and spilled out head first, scraping the skin off her face on some crusty snow. Skiing was cold and wet. Diane convinced Steve that she probably would have hated it even if she were able-bodied.

Next they tried swimming in the pool at McKay-Dee Hospital in Ogden where he worked. Diane felt more at home in the water. A ski belt around the waist helped her with balance, and she soon found herself paddling around on her back. But when she tried the front crawl, she couldn't pull hard enough with her arms to get her head out of the water. Then she couldn't turn back on her back. She started to panic, thrashing in the water, trying desperately to get air. Where was Steve? Finally, she went limp and had nearly passed out when Steve suddenly flipped her over and held her tightly in his arms.

"What were you going to do? Let me drown here?" she gasped.

"I'm sorry. I wanted to see if you could do it yourself."

He kissed the corner of each eye. He tasted the salt water of her tears. "You're crying. I'm so sorry."

After a while, with his help, Diane could twist her arms and shoulders to turn herself over. From then on, she felt a freedom she had not known since the accident. She eliminated the ski belt and did somersaults in the water, both forward and back.

"What would I do if you weren't paralyzed?" asked Steve, laughing. "I couldn't keep up with you! You're a fish."

Diane was happy in the water with Steve. He reminded her of Johnny, of course, but circumstances were so different. Steve wasn't the champion. Instead, he made her feel like one.

Diane swam back to the electric pool lift that had taken her into the water from her wheelchair. She rode it back out, transferred to her wheelchair, and went to the deep end of the pool. Steve waited for her as she gathered courage and finally pitched forward out of her chair, head first into the water. She came up smoothly into his arms.

"Good girl," he said. It was Diane's favorite compliment.

Crocuses had barely awakened in the spring before Steve took Diane hiking, carrying her on his back. They went boating and fishing with his family. With Steve, Diane felt young and alive once more.

Her first year of teaching school ended in May. One by one the children came to hug her good-bye. She was their teacher, and they were the tangible, flesh-and-blood evidence of her greatest success. Diane's mom had come to help clear her things from the room. As Diane watched the last of the children run out the door, she turned and buried her face in her mother's skirt.

"Oh, Mom. It's so hard to let them go," she sobbed.

"I know, Diane," said her mom. "How well I know."

One evening at a party, Diane overheard someone talking to Steve. "You'd better think about this, buddy. I think you're falling for her. Don't do anything you'll regret!"

Diane was angry and mortified at the same time. Was Steve really falling in love with her? Later, she told him what she had heard and said, "It's good advice, Steve. Marriage is hard enough without the wheelchair and my condition being an issue. Promise me you'll think about it."

"I promise."

A few days later, Steve said to her, "I can't believe they let you out of rehab so dependent on others. Maybe somebody else with your injury wouldn't be able to do everything, but you're an athlete. You're light and not that uncoordinated. You need to go back and find out what you've got. You really ought to practice what you preach and start giving one hundred percent of yourself."

Diane could always count on Steve for blunt honesty. Because he had shown her so many of her possibilities, Diane accepted his challenge. In spite of her dread of old memories of the place, she arranged with Doctor Swenson to go back to the University of Utah Rehabilitation Center for an extended stay. Steve triggered in her the old spark to once again be the best she could be.

That summer, Diane Ellingson, former gymnastics champion, was once again involved in intensive training, this time to learn some of the basic skills of infants, many of which are impossible for most quadriplegics. In fact, she tried to pattern herself after babies, picturing in her mind the endless patience with which they try repeatedly to learn a skill. This time she wasn't expecting to master five new tricks a day.

It was not her lame body that Diane most wanted to conquer, but her hands. Theoretically, because she could sit up on a flat surface and transfer to the wheelchair, she should have been able to dress herself, but to gracefully maneuver the little things that make clothes practical requires supple fingers. Buttons, zippers, ribbons, hooks and eyes, snaps, shoelaces, buckles, and straps were still enemies to Diane's stiff, uncooperative fingers. She first put hours of thought into how to adapt herself to meet these common, simple foes. Then she spent days fumbling around and feeling clumsy, but she was finally able to trap and manipulate things between both hands or with her teeth. With the help of her mother and occupational therapist, she had ribbon loops sewn onto her elastic socks, reinforced belt loops put on her pants, and she learned to use a button hook made out of stout wire. Finally, she dressed herself for the first time.

It was like costuming a department store dummy. She sat in the wheelchair to wriggle into her shirt, turning from side to side to get it straight. She pulled her special elastic stockings up over limp feet and legs and with looped velcro straps secured her leg bag so that it would be hidden against the inside of her leg. Transferring to a wide, flat table, she slowly forced her lifeless legs, inch by inch, down into her pant legs and then lay down to pull the pants up to her waist. She rested for a while before stuffing her shirt into the waistband of her pants. Finally she sat up again to transfer to the wheelchair to pull on her shoes. It had taken an hour to do all that.

"I can't believe I waited so long to try!" She laughed, as she hugged her therapist. "I've decided that there isn't anything I can't do if I can just figure out how to adapt things to make it work."

"That's the ticket."

"Is it possible for a quad to transfer from the floor to the chair?"

"I don't know of any who can, but if you want, we can see what we can figure out."

They tried several techniques used by paraplegics, such as pulling up from bars, to get Diane from the floor, but without grip in her fingers, it was impossible for her to do. In trying that, however, it became obvious that Diane wasn't strong, so she started doing bar dips between parallel bars and taking endurance runs in her wheelchair around the hospital and along the sidewalks outside. She learned to jump small curbs and manage cracks in the pavement, and she was ecstatic to think that she would never get trapped again as she had that day outside the elementary school.

At last, one day while the therapists and the other patients in the room urged her on, with only the strength in her biceps and some in her triceps and shoulders, Diane dragged her own dead weight, inch by inch, the marathon distance of three feet up from the floor into her wheelchair. She struggled, rested, and struggled again for more than an hour until finally, groaning with exhaustion and shaking with muscle fatigue, she made that last twisting turn to a full sitting position. Everyone cheered when Diane threw her arms high above her head in a victory salute, flashing that famous Ellingson smile.

"I used to call myself a 'spaz' when I had trouble doing something in gymnastics," she said. "Boy, do I regret ever using that word. It's so unfair."

Diane's only requirement for herself to graduate from this

self-imposed school was to get herself up, manage her own bowel and bladder care, and shower and dress — for the average woman, an easy ritual that takes about three-quarters of an hour.

On the last day in rehab, Diane woke, rolled over, and sat up. That was a major fight against gravity, which initiated the usual violent spasming in her body that lasted about thirty seconds. After resting from that, she transferred to her wheelchair to go into the bathroom where she washed and sterilized her leg bag and transferred herself to the toilet. Then she had to transfer back to the wheelchair, transfer again onto a special shower chair, shower, and transfer back to her wheelchair once more to dry herself. An hour and a half was gone, and she was exhausted. She remembered the first time, just a couple of weeks ago, when she learned to make that series of transfers. It had been the first time in three years that she had taken a shower in privacy.

Then she dressed herself in just under an hour.

During the four years since her injury, Diane had perfected the skills of styling her hair, brushing her teeth, and putting on her makeup, all of which she could do in thirty minutes. But the rest of the regimen would always be a slow process. For the rest of her life she would rise at 4:00 to start her day, spending three and a half hours doing what others do in a few minutes. But when she left rehab that day with this new level of independence, Diane knew that she had gone for the gold and won.

Chapter 20

Diane returned home from rehab feeling triumphant and renewed and optimistic about her own strengths. But there was bitter along with the sweet. In her absence Steve had involved himself heavily in school and no longer saw her every day. When they were together, their relationship seemed strained. Diane knew they should talk, and she knew Steve knew it too, but neither said anything, as if silence were the perfect denial. After a few weeks, Steve went camping for a week. The day he returned, he and Diane drove along Foothill Boulevard and stopped at a spot overlooking the valley. He had a beard. He looked different. Diane knew he was different.

"I don't know if I like it," she said as he scooted her over to him. She rubbed her cheek against his, surprised by the softness of the beard and delighted by the warmth of his touch. "I might be able to get used to it," she whispered.

His shoulders stiffened, and Diane's heart clenched. A

long moment passed before she could trust her voice. Then she said, "Something's changed, hasn't it?"

"Yes."

Diane felt the inevitable sadness of clarifying the truth. She owed Steve so much. She loved him for opening up the world to her, but she could admit what she had suspected, even before she returned to rehab. Steve was slipping away.

"Diane, you are a great person. You're beautiful and funny and smart. You'll make a terrific wife."

"But not for you."

"No."

Diane buried her face into his shoulder and said, "Oh, Steve, I'm independent now."

He hugged her tightly, their tears mingling together as they clung to one another.

"I thought we loved each other. What happened?"

"I don't know."

That night alone, Diane pondered her feelings. Going back to rehab had made her less emotionally dependent on Steve. It was a bitter but valid truth that when Steve quit work as a nurse at the end of the day, he wanted to leave it all behind, not go home to it. Diane knew that her independence was the key to unlocking his obligation to her. In spite of losing him, she had gained pride in her accomplishments, and she once again felt the intangible, delicious confidence of the athlete. She would always be grateful to him for that, and the two remained good friends.

When school started again in the fall, Diane and Marie decided to move into an apartment together. They looked at dozens of ground-floor places but soon became discouraged, realizing that there was nothing for the handicapped. Cupboards and counters were too high, doorways were too narrow, bathrooms were too small. Finally, Diane considered building her own home.

She and her parents flew to New York to establish her disability status with the insurance company, Murphy and Beane. While there, they discussed with Mr. O'Boyle the possibility of building a house. With her parents cosigning, the company agreed to match her savings for a down payment on a handicapped-efficient home. Diane worked over the figures on paper and determined that if she budgeted her money carefully and made double payments, she could and would pay off the house in a little more than five years. It was a goal she vowed to reach.

The trip to New York had been very difficult. She had had to notify the airline in advance of her special needs. A steward met her at the gate. He took her out of her own wheelchair and put her in a very narrow chair specially made to fit in the aisle of the airplane. Once they were inside the plane, he lifted her to her seat. Meanwhile, her wheelchair was stowed in the belly of the plane with the luggage. She was nervous about that, realizing that if the chair got lost when they changed planes in Chicago, she would be totally helpless. The constant transferring, waiting in the airport, being transported to and from the hotel, and then having to adjust to the strange, inconvenient facilities of the hotel room, were exhausting for her as well as for her parents. Diane had to bring an extra suitcase just for her supplies. It was obvious that she would never be able to travel alone.

Ironically, soon after she returned home from that trip, Darol Wagstaff informed her that he could book several speaking engagements for her out of state. Diane's second career as a motivational speaker was taking off, and it was inevitable that she would be flying again. She decided to hire Marie to be her traveling companion. It turned out to be a perfect match. Marie was unflappable in making the thousand and one necessary arrangements for travel, she was strong and capable of handling Diane's physical needs, and she was full of wit and charm with strangers.

On Easter Sunday, Diane woke for the first time in her own new house. Supremely comfortable with satisfaction, she lay thinking about her life. Her second year of teaching had been perfect. The children touched her so deeply with their innocence, and she knew that she had touched them. One of her students told her that he had been afraid to have her for a teacher because she was in a wheelchair, but she had turned out to be his favorite. Diane smiled to herself, remembering her principal telling her that she had the best disciplined class in the school. If only he could have seen me student teaching, she thought.

Diane remembered the Easter four years before when she left rehab for her first visit home. It had been so frightening. Now, here she was contented and happy in her home—*her* home, decorated in country blue and pink, furnished to accommodate her wheelchair, designed by herself to fit her every need. Images of the nightmare of the first few months long ago in the hospital flashed through her mind, but she quickly chased them away. That was how she maintained her optimism, by refusing to allow negative thoughts of any kind to enter her mind. She never let herself hit rock bottom again. That horrible day when she was injured was no more to her than a vague, faded old photograph shut away in some dusty family album. It was there, but she didn't have to look at it.

Diane yawned and stretched, deciding that it was time to get going for the day. She had her Sunday School lesson to teach that morning, a family dinner at her parents' home in the afternoon, and a special devotional to speak at in the evening. There was plenty of time to get ready, but she resolutely threw the floral comforter away from her. She had something she was determined to accomplish this morning, and during the night it had come to her how she might do it.

After showering and dressing, she sat in front of the mirror, took a deep breath, and began. First, she trapped the earring between the knuckles of the index and middle fingers of her right hand and adjusted it for a good, firm hold with her teeth. Then, by holding her earlobe taut with the same fingers of her left hand, she poked, poked, dropped the earring, picked it up, poked and poked again until finally, after twenty minutes, she got the post through the hole in her earlobe. Her arms were tired and her neck ached with the effort, but the earring was in. The real problem, however, was getting the back onto the post. She had tried it a hundred times, but because it was so tiny, she had always given up and called her mother.

Today, though, she tried her secret weapon, the idea for which had come from watching her kids at school. She dug out a glob of Silly Putty from its plastic egg and stuck it on the knuckle of the index finger of her left hand. Then she picked up the tiny gold earring back with her tongue and positioned it firmly in the pliable plastic mass. She guided her knuckle behind her ear, held the front still against the fingers of her other hand, and proceeded blindly to try to make the back connect with the post. The minutes ticked by as she moved it around and around. Then, suddenly, she felt the back catch and slip into place.

Ecstasy! It had taken her forty minutes to put in one earring, and she was giddy with the accomplishment. She rested for a few minutes before tackling the other ear. This time it was easier, now that she knew what to do. In the next few weeks, she would get the maneuver down to a cold ten minutes.

That evening, Diane sat before her audience of young people feeling especially good. Putting in earrings might be a small thing to others, but it was a major triumph to her. She had long ago learned to savor the small, beautiful joys of life. Having learned to tie a hair ribbon with her hooked fingers, for instance, was another of her secret vanities. She sat in her crisply ironed, flowered dress, a perfect blue ribbon accenting the piles of gold blonde hair that flowed in waves over her shoulders, knowing that her makeup was perfect — all of this the effect of hours of patient struggle. No one could know what it had cost for her to feel confident and beautiful tonight.

When her turn came to speak, she wheeled to the front and looked out over the young faces. She pitied the discomfort in their eyes as they instinctively tried to avoid staring at her wheelchair. She would set them at ease, as she always did. Giving them her famous smile she said, "I appreciate that beautiful vocal solo we just heard. You're lucky I didn't come here to sing to you. People say I sing about as well as I walk."

Laughter. That was the idea. Her talks always started out that way. She then proceeded to lure them into the story of her earlier gymnastics life, making them understand the great cost of fame by taking them with her to the top of the victory stand and then to the bottom with her defeats. She told them her favorite stories of the time she blew her chance at nationals when she looked at that boy and fell off the beam twice and then later came down in a belly flop from her dismount on the bars. She told them that she wanted to quit, that she thought all those years of training had been for nothing. She had never attended an after-school activity, had never been to a football game. Then she related the words of the great Nancy Theis that to quit was the only failure. To get up and try again was success. She told of going on to one more gymnastics meet and ending up United States Junior Olympic gold medal champion.

"As I took my place on the top step of the victory stand under an arch of red roses, I received a national title and a giant trophy. How thankful I was that I had found the courage to get back up, to try one more time, because that day I went home the winner. The national champion. I made a promise to myself that day. No matter how hard I fall, no matter how many times I fail in my life, I will never, ever give up."

By that time, her listeners held her in awe. They were not seeing a pitiful girl in a wheelchair but a champion athlete. Then, just when they could most feel the joy of triumph, she carried them crashing to the mat of despair.

"Just two days into my professional gymnastics tour, tragedy struck. I overrotated a somersault from the vaulting horse and landed on the back of my neck. The vertebrae were fractured, the spinal cord was damaged, and my career as a professional gymnast was traded for life in a wheelchair.

"Words can't express the pain and the sorrow that come into your life when something like that happens. How thankful I was for friends and family who surrounded me with love and tried to encourage me to go on. I remember, soon after my recovery in the hospital, I was sitting at home in a wheelchair looking at my reflection in a full-length mirror. I didn't see the graceful form of a nationally ranked gymnast. I saw the broken, crippled body of a stranger. At that point I knew that I had two choices. Give up or get up. I had lost everything in the world. Nobody would blame me if I quit. But my mind wandered back to a victory stand under an arch of roses, and a promise that I would never, ever give up.

"Every person in this room has struggles and challenges that are every bit as real to them as mine are to me." Suddenly, tears filled Diane's eyes. She had given this speech hundreds of times, yet tonight she felt herself wandering in the minds of the teenagers who sat before her, feeling their fears and anxiety, sensing the tenderness of their hopes.

"If there's one message that I could give to you tonight," she continued, "it would be to realize your potential and have faith to wait while you work for your dreams to come true."

It was no use. She could see the hesitancy in some of their faces. She had been just like them, crazy to grab it all at once, unwilling to wait for anything. Life would grind away at them and bow their heads a bit. Some would look up, however, and believe in their dreams, others would keep looking down. Some would live lives of inspiration; others of desperation.

She smiled. Perhaps there was already someone out there who was suffering the poignant, heartbreaking hopelessness of a personal tragedy. If she could reach just that one person. There was only one real message she could give. She had learned it from the people she most admired in life. From her parents. From Nancy Theis and Michelle and Paul and Greg. God had spoken it to her that night when she threw her burdens on him and he gladly took them up.

Diane suddenly wished she could leap up and pound on the pulpit like a revivalist preacher. She wished she could run out into that crowd of people and somehow infuse them with the message.

She immediately reprimanded herself for the wish. God didn't intend it to be that way. He had said, "I . . . show forth my wisdom through the weak things of the earth" (D&C 124:1). He had also said, "If they humble themselves before me, and have faith in me, then will I make weak things become strong unto them." (Ether 12:27.)

Diane felt strong. Her life was not tragic. It was magic. She gave the crowd her most persuasive argument, that beautiful Ellingson smile, and told them the secret.

"Never give up," she said. "Don't you DARE give up!"